Eleven Plus without the Fuss

A Parents' Guide to Secondary School Selection: National Edition

Anita and Tim Hill

Onwards and Upwards Publishers

Berkeley House,
11 Nightingale Crescent,
Leatherhead,
Surrey,
KT24 6PD.

www.onwardsandupwards.org

Printed in the UK.

ISBN: 978-1-910197-15-8
Cover design: Leah-Maarit

Dedication

To Alicia and Joshua.

We are so proud of you.

Acknowledgments

A big thank you to all the experts, teachers and parents who have contributed articles to this book, whether in name or anonymously. You know who you are, and your input has been invaluable. Thanks to Diane - if it were not for you Anita would never have started her tutoring services. Particular thanks must also go to Christabel and Marilyn for your support, advice, encouragement and friendship. Thank you to the staff of Eleven Plus Exams and of Zoom Photography in Kingston. You bought into our vision and helped enrich this book. Thanks also to Mark and Diana. You believed in us from day one and you made all this possible. Finally, a massive thank you and big hugs to our children for helping us learn all about the school selection process from a parents' viewpoint, for giving us time to work on this project and simply for being such brilliant, talented and fun kids. We are really proud of you, and we love you loads.

Anita and Tim Hill
Claygate, Surrey, March 2015

Contents

About the Authors

Anita Hill started her teaching career in 1990 and in 1992 became a Head of Department in a large West London state comprehensive school. Since having her own children she has become a primary school teacher in north east Surrey and in addition has been tutoring verbal and non-verbal reasoning techniques for 10 years. She has a high success rate with children gaining places in all of the local selective secondary schools in both the state and private sectors. She gives help and encouragement to parents and pupils alike and this book is a distillation of much that she has learned through her tutoring services, enabling her to offer a wider group of parents support and advice based on the benefit of her experience. She was educated in the state grammar system and, briefly, in the independent sector. She is a state school teacher herself, currently teaching in a primary school. She has a Music in Education degree and a PGCE in secondary education.

Tim Hill is an experienced digital strategy consultant and project manager. Throughout his career he has held sales, marketing and consulting roles for companies such as IBM, CSC and British Telecom as well as smaller, specialist e-commerce and software development organisations. He currently runs his own consulting business and, for the last twelve years, has in addition held visiting senior lecturer positions at two London universities, teaching business and computing subjects. He was educated in the state comprehensive system. He has a Masters degree in Information Systems as well as multiple professional qualifications and accreditations. In his spare time he can be found trying to fix up old cars or playing electric guitar.

Anita and Tim have a daughter and son who are at schools in Surrey and both children have benefited from state and independent education. They live in Esher in Surrey.

Foreword

This is a book for our time. Its purpose is to enable parents to navigate their way through an increasingly complex educational system, in order to make an informed choice in one of the most important decisions that they will make for their child – which secondary school?

The character of schools has always of course been of interest to the discerning parent. Parents often talk to others about the merits of local schools, particularly at those crucial times when their offspring are about to transfer from one stage of schooling to another. Schools sometimes acquire 'reputations' for being 'good' or 'bad' in general or specific terms. The keen interest in reputations indicates that parents firmly believe that schools can confer advantages or disadvantages on those who attend them. In other words, choice of school matters!

The last three decades can be seen as one of the most intensive periods of change in the history of the education system. Change has continued unabated to the present day. It has resulted in the centralisation of the curriculum, national testing, league tables, the creation of alternative types of schools inside and outside the maintained sector, and a dramatic reduction in the responsibilities of LEAs.

Over 90% of primary school children will transfer to secondary state schools, of which there are four main kinds: Community, Foundation & Trust, Voluntary Aided and Voluntary Controlled. In addition to these there are City Technology Colleges, Free Schools, Grammar Schools, Faith Schools, and Specialist Academies – a bewildering choice! There is a wealth of information available to parents about these different types of state secondary schools on various government websites. However, many parents of children in state primary schools are unaware of the range of independent schools in their locality, whether their child might be eligible to apply, and more crucially, how to prepare them for the 11+ or Common Entrance exams.

As the former headteacher of a Voluntary Aided primary school I saw it as part of my role to advise parents of pupils at the beginning of Year 5, of the types of schools available, what questions they might ask on Open Days and I explained the application processes to both state and independent secondary schools. However, my experience as an Ofsted Inspector inspecting primary schools across the country was that guidance for parents on the transition to Secondary School was often ad hoc.

What this book does very effectively is to extend the general information available to parents, about possible choices of school, to include independent schools (also known as 'private schools'). By equipping parents with valuable insights and guidance, hints about how to spot good leadership, the right questions to ask at Open Days and advice about assisted places, the authors speak with authority and credibility. With many years' experience of successfully tutoring children in Surrey to gain entry to local grammar and independent schools, Anita Hill has creditable experience in this sphere.

I am also particularly heartened by the inclusion of the 'Missing Piece' section of the book and it contains advice we could all use from time to time! Parents sometimes get terribly worked up about their child's progress, and usually the child senses this, which is ultimately counter-productive. Yes, school applications are important, but a secure, well-adjusted child from a happy, nurturing environment will make the world a better place regardless of educational background.

By taking the fuss out of eleven plus and making this knowledge available to a wider range of parents in state primary schools, Anita and Tim Hill will have empowered them to access, from an informed position, the most suitable secondary school for their child. I urge headteachers and governors to also read this book and to consider how they might use it to support and inform parents and prepare pupils who are in the process of transition to secondary school.

Christabel McLean-Bacchus, MA (Ed)
(Headteacher and Ofsted Additional Inspector - retired)

Within each of us, just waiting to blossom, is the wonderful promise of all that we can be – Anonymous.

Introduction

Having gone through the selective secondary school application and selection process as parents, as well as Anita's ten years as a tutor, we understand first-hand the stresses that many parents can feel about the 11+ exam system. It is an inherently competitive situation with children often battling for a finite number of places at over-subscribed schools. Hence parents tend inevitably to be secretive about their particular approach to tutoring, who they use, when they start and exactly how intensively they prepare the child. We have seen the concern and confusion in, for example, year 4 parents totally daunted by the prospect of navigating their way through the maze of possibilities, desperate to get their child into an appropriate school, yet all the while bombarded on every side by very strongly held and contradictory opinions voiced by self-proclaimed experts at class coffee mornings, dinner parties and any number of social gatherings.

This book is therefore intended to address that need as well as being a response to the increasing number of "Help!" phone-calls that Anita has had from panicked parents not realising that their child will need to undertake a verbal and non-verbal exam in a matter of weeks - even days sometimes - and they don't know what this entails.

Eleven Plus without the Fuss is a book for families who are looking for their children to change schools at age 11 (or 13 as there is often a pre-test at 11). Parents do not always know what type of school they want until they go through this process which is why we have included discussions and information about a wide range of schools including state, private, selective, non-selective, co-ed and single sex. A parent may want to look into schools in the independent sector just because that is what the majority of their friends are considering, but in fact the state sector may be the right choice for them.

Sometimes it becomes obvious by year 4 that a child is not achieving as well as expected. Development, like growth, can only be predicted so far. Boys in particular may take longer to develop. You must have heard parents say, "… he's a bit behind - or maybe it's that he's just a boy!" Boys tend to find it harder to sit still when they are little so some take longer to start focussing in lessons and, therefore, learning. It may be important to take a more detailed look at your child and see if there is a learning difficulty, perhaps dyslexia or a processing issue, and information about this is included. Maybe your child is not ready to move to a secondary school and be a small fish in a large pond at this point in his/her development and would benefit from being in the top end of a prep school. Some years ago state education preferred the 'middle' school environment and in many geographical areas this continues. Anita's observation, born of many years of experience, is that, money permitting, for some children it is better to move in year 5 to a prep school and although it is likely that they will still need to take the 11+/12+ pre-test, the prep school will prepare your child and select an appropriate high school for them. They will then take the 'Common Entrance' and having reached the required mark will then go to this school.

Regions where there is high demand for independent school places are, for the most part, affluent areas where a large number of parents are well-educated professionals and generally they know what they think (if they don't know they can usually 'Google' the answers). *Eleven Plus Without the Fuss* provides most of the information in one place and gives the intelligent, thinking parent some pointers to consider. As they are published, further regional editions will contain information about the various local schools.

Part A of the book gives the broader background to choosing a school with the help of experts including headteachers and subject experts discussing issues such as choosing a secondary school, spotting effective leadership and management in schools, league tables, what is meant by 'Value Added', the pros and cons of single sex education and information about scholarships and bursaries.

If you are intending for your child to be tutored (frankly for selective schools most do) then this section will also help you understand how to choose a tutor and give you some insight into what preparation your child will need in order to be in a competitive position ready for the entrance exams.

In Part B we introduce parents and pupils to verbal and non-verbal reasoning. You may wish to try and take your child through the

11+ preparation process yourself and in which case you can cut these pages out (or not) and take them to restaurants as puzzles to do – they won't know the difference! If you are not going to use a professional tutor then contact us through the website (**www.elevateeleven.com**) for further support and guidance.

Part C is based on interview preparation, with sample interview questions to use at home around the dinner table or at Christmas parties as well as hints and tips on giving a good impression.

Part C also includes some removable, 'cut-out-and-keep' parent & pupil planners to keep you going through what can be quite an intensive phase of life. Also included are Anita's tried and tested tutoring action plans… 11+ in 11 months, 11+ in 11 weeks and 11+ at the 11th hour.

Part D, 'The Missing Piece', encourages us all to keep it in perspective as it is all too easy for parents (and children) to get caught up in this all-consuming process that can totally dominate and take over a year or more of their lives. It should not be like that and, for example, there is a lovely article from a friend who wanted to escape it all, took her children travelling and her son sat the school entrance exam with almost no preparation at all.

Part E is designed to help you understand more about the choices available to you, regardless of where you live. In addition, if you are reading a 'regionalised' edition of this book then Part E also contains the localised 'Schools Directory', so that as far as possible all core information you need about the local schools is collated into a single, accessible resource. We have provided details about fees, exam content, etc. Note that we are not giving our personal opinions about which schools are best. That is for you to decide. We are sticking to public-domain facts and what the schools say about themselves to avoid you having to ask the same basic questions ten times over!

We are based in the north east Surrey area and, as well as our weekly after-school tutoring classes that continue to run throughout the year, we have developed a consulting business to help guide parents through the process. If you feel that you would benefit from this please contact us through the website or email us using the contact details at the end of this book.

WHY 'ELEVATE ELEVEN?'

The 11+ process will be a journey which will elevate your child intellectually but it can also develop their character. Elevate can mean to 'raise to a higher intellectual or spiritual level'. For our family it *was* a spiritual experience as well as an intellectual one and we have included some reflective quotes which could be helpful for your 10-year olds and also make good discussion points, as for many of your children these will be their first significant exams.

As well as 11 being the age that many children transfer to secondary school - just think – Apollo 11 was the mission that put the first man on the moon! You never know where this process will take you. And if it is the 11th hour for you – it may be your final opportunity to act but it is not necessarily too late to develop these skills.

On the Elevate Eleven website (**www.elevateeleven.com**) we have included downloadable materials and information about other related services that we offer – secondary school transfer workshops for year 5 and 6 pupils to help deal with worries about school transfer and pressure of exams. We will also continue to update the news section as often as it is relevant, with details of school exam dates. We will be running mock exams and practice computer-based tests in our area in association with **www.elevenplusexams.co.uk** and the website will contain the latest information about these.

Believe with all your heart that you will do what you were made to do
— Orison Swett Marsden

A. Navigating the Maze

'The right school can transform children's lives and help
them achieve things that they may have never imagined.'
Department of Education

Where Do I Start?

We expect the reason you have picked up this book is because
you are embarking on the exciting journey of choosing a secondary
school. Maybe you think that 'stressful' or 'confusing' are better
adjectives to describe this process. We imagine that you feel that you
have several options, which is why you are reading this!

If, like us, you live in an area that still has the state grammar
school system, your choices are more complex and may involve
strategic decisions about extra tutoring a year or more before school
application submission deadlines. Furthermore if you have the
financial means to consider private education (and don't forget
bursaries and scholarships) then you also have options open to you
about when to transfer your child from one school to another. For
example, you might choose to move your child at age 9 or even at 11
to the preparatory ('prep') system and then again at 13 via 'common
entrance'. Note that financial assistance is rare in the prep schools but
widely offered by secondary schools – see information about bursaries
and scholarships.

ASK LOTS OF QUESTIONS

Children develop differently and parents want different things –
this is often coloured by our own educational backgrounds, and when
Mum wants one thing and Dad another, discussions need to be had. In
my consultancy business we help parents along this journey by
analysing their aspirations and the child's needs with a view to
suggesting certain schools. To an extent you can do this yourselves by
asking some key questions.

It helps if you know how your child is performing at school. What are their national curriculum attainment levels right now, and how are they progressing? Some selective schools will say whether your child will need level 4 or 5 in Maths by year 6. Are they in the top groups? Do they struggle with anything in particular? What is their passion?

Some parents do not realise that bursaries and assisted places are available as well as scholarships, so do not discount private education immediately if you think that you may want it but may not be able to afford it. One hundred per cent bursaries really do exist.

VISIT LOTS OF SCHOOLS

At the back of regional versions of this book we have listed all the prep schools and selective secondary schools in the local area so this may be of use to you if we cover where you live. Wherever you are in the country, once you are clearer about what you want and have made an initial shortlist, have a look at the school websites and visit them on their 'open days'. However, do not rely on your 12 year old 'tour guide' to give you all the answers that you require. They may feel under pressure or intimidated by you and make something up! It has been known. You may be able to reduce the number of individual visits by going along to a 'schools fair' where multiple schools are represented in the same place. There are some such events in London and other major cities but any larger prep school near you may host their own as a way of supporting and advising parents of children at that school. They will generally allow parents from other schools to come along as well so contact any such local school to see if they are going to host one of these events.

You may also be able to book a parent tour of any individual school. It is a good idea to see a school during a normal school day and not just at an open day. Look at the work on the walls and how attentive and polite the children are. If you are shown around by the headteacher or member of the senior management team you may be able to ask those more in depth, probing questions. The article by Alison Taylor will give you further ideas of what to look for.

If you have decided to apply for state schools, whether grammar or mixed ability, you need to consider catchment areas. The schools will let you know the boundaries of the catchment area for previous years. Do not presume that you will get into your local school unless of course you live next door and remember that catchment area limits are usually based on an 'as the crow flies' measurement and not on the basis of driving or walking distance. So, if in doubt, get the information from the schools, buy a map, a ruler and a pair of compasses! If you cannot work out how to convert distance into the right scale for the map then your child probably can! You may want to consider a specialist school a bit further away if they target talented children and your child has a particular ability.

All children in year 6 will be provided with a booklet by the local education authority listing the state schools in the area. This will help you with your state school choice. If you are considering selective grammar or private schools then you need to start deciding earlier as tutoring for these generally starts early in year 5. You also need to find out what the entrance exams consist of as you don't want to pay for non-verbal reasoning tutoring only to then discover that the school only tests verbal reasoning acumen.

The Basic Problem

Education stories always hit the headlines. The following article from the Daily Telegraph, although somewhat sensationalistic, graphically illustrates the basic problem parents face and is probably in part why you are reading this book:

School admissions: half of pupils rejected in some towns
Source: **www.telegraph.co.uk**, March 1st, 2012

Just 24 hours after state school allocations were made across England, it emerged that tens of thousands of 11-year-

olds have been given second, third or fourth choice comprehensives. In some towns and cities, children missed out on as many as six secondary schools. An analysis of council data shows that the rejection rate is being driven by competition to get into grammar schools and a new generation of independent academies and free schools.

In Slough, Berkshire, almost six-in-10 children – 59 per cent – were rejected from their first choice school, compared with 54 per cent a year ago. A third of pupils missed out on at least three schools. The local council admitted the rejection rate was high compared with other areas but insisted it reflected the "high number of grammar school places available in the town".

Councils in London also reported that large numbers of pupils were rejected. Across the capital's 33 boroughs, a third of children on average failed to secure their favoured school, while one-in-20 missed out on at least six – the maximum number of choices in London. In Wandsworth, 46.5 per cent of pupils failed to secure their favoured school, while numbers were as high as 45.5 per cent in Hammersmith and Fulham, 44 per cent in Southwark and 43 per cent in Kensington and Chelsea. It comes as data shows that some of London's academies and free schools – independent institutions free of council control – received up to nine applications for every place.

Siobhan Freegard, co-founder of parenting website Netmums, said: "We are seeing more areas around the UK becoming increasingly short on secondary school places."

The sheer scale of rejections in some cities is likely to lead to a sharp rise in the number of parents lodging official appeals. Matt Richards, of schoolappeals.com, said rising demand for the best state schools is "probably down to people who can't afford private school anymore".

Under a new admissions code – introduced for the first time this year – mothers and fathers are given 20 days to challenge school allocations, twice the original timeframe. He said:

"What we're noticing this year are far more parents willing to go down that road [to an appeal] because they don't want the comprehensive, they want the good grammar."

Last year, almost one-in-six children were turned away from their first choice school. Yesterday, the Telegraph obtained data from 50 local authorities – a third of those nationally. In almost six-in-10 council areas, more pupils secured their first choice school this year compared with 2011. It is likely to be down to a drop in the number of applications in many areas caused by falling school rolls. A further quarter of councils reported a decline in the number of 11-year-olds gaining their first choice, while numbers remained the same in other areas.

Local authorities including Manchester, Poole, Trafford, Southend-on-Sea, Wokingham and Wolverhampton reported that at least a fifth of pupils missed their preferred secondary school. The largest number of first choices was recorded in Cornwall, Derbyshire, Hartlepool, Herefordshire, the Isle of Wight, North Somerset, St Helens and Tameside, where at least 98 per cent of pupils gained their preferred school.

We do not wish to drum up hysteria here. The truth is that the actual data, once the dust has settled, will be significantly better. Children who apply for private school places also apply for state places. Those that take up a private place will therefore relinquish their place in the state queue and hence someone who did not initially get their first choice will then find that they are offered it after all. Buried in the gloom of the article is some good news too. Parents now have double the number of days to appeal - increased from ten days to twenty - and this is well worth doing. We know of many people who have appealed successfully in the past.

CUNNING PARENTS

Because it has become so difficult to get into first choice schools the savvy parent has learned how to play the game to their advantage – sometimes unethically or even illegally. Families move house well in advance of secondary education into catchment areas for 'good' schools, they go to church more to get their children into faith schools and even use grandparents' addresses or names of other children with the same surname as siblings, and so on, in order to cheat the system. Councils are wising up to this last point, and parents have been successfully prosecuted, so aside from the moral issues it is simply a risk not worth taking.

Houses in good catchment areas are becoming more expensive, and therefore the system is increasingly weighted in favour of the wealthy middle-classes. This has tended to have a 'vicious-circle' effect, with parents desperate to keep their children away from schools full of 'undesirables' and hence will move heaven and earth to get their child into the *right school*, whatever they think that means. This enhances still further the perception of which schools are good or bad, and the circle is completed for another year.

The hard truth is that many parents will do all they can to play the system and sail as close to the wind as they think they can get away with. If you are applying for secondary schools for your children then, like it or not, that is the contest you are joining and it is not an entirely level playing field. You don't make the rules and some people do not play fairly.

This book is all about helping you to understand the rules of the game and how to exploit them legitimately. Finding the right school is time-consuming but you also need considerable knowledge. We are hoping to help you here by putting the basic information that you will need into one place.

Types of School

Let's start with types of state school. As well as grammar schools (academically selective) and mixed-ability secondary schools (not normally selective) there are a number of other varieties and subdivisions as follows:

- **Faith Schools** - Faith schools often appear higher in the league tables. With some families fabricating their involvement in a church many schools seek proof of attendance and, for example, Catholic schools insist on certificates of baptism and evidence from the priest of regular attendance at mass. Faith schools vary considerably in the degree to which they feature their particular religious viewpoint on a day-to-day basis within school life;

- **Free Schools** - Free schools are becoming inundated with applications well before the doors are actually opened. These schools are state funded but are independent of government control and the Local Education Authority. They devise their own curriculum, length of school day and holidays. They do not take a 'one size fits all' approach and respond to specific parental demands;

- **Specialist status schools** - These are schools that have a specialism such as science or music. It was a government initiative that encouraged secondary schools in England to specialise in certain areas of the curriculum in order to 'boost achievement';

- **Academies** - An 'academy' sounds grand, but in reality it is a school that is state-maintained with the help of outside sponsors. Originally, they were called city academies, but the name was changed to enable the creation of academies in the rural areas. Just because a school is an academy does not mean it is any better or worse than any other school as it is largely a label relating to how the school is funded.

New Admissions Code 2012

The Department for Education published a new School Admissions Code on 1 February 2012. Section 1.32 states that where tests are used for selection Admission authorities must, *"take all reasonable steps to inform parents of the outcome of selection tests before the closing date for secondary applications on 31 October so as to allow parents time to make an informed choice of school – while making clear that this does not equate to a guarantee of a selective place"*.

The knock-on effect of this is that the entrance exams for selective schools have become earlier to accommodate this date, often now being as early as September. The advantage for most people is that you will have an idea of whether your child is likely to get into that school and can happily complete the Common Application Form for your local schools. If it is unlikely that your child will get into the selective school then you can use that place on the form for another school. For some schools there will be a further test to continue the selection process.

This is what Tiffin Girls' School (a selective state grammar) in Kingston said as a result of these changes:

> ...the Governors of Tiffin Girls' School have decided that the entrance tests for entry to Year 7 in September 2013 will be a two stage process.
>
> Stage 1 will consist of the same style non-verbal and verbal reasoning papers as in our current arrangements and will be the same test as that offered by The Tiffin School. The date of this test will be 27th September 2012. The candidates who score the same mark as the 400th candidate and above will be invited to sit the tests that form Stage 2 of the process which will take place on Saturday 8th December 2012.
>
> Parents will be told of the outcome of Stage 1 in time to inform them as to whether or not to name the school on the Common Application Form. Candidates who score a lower mark than the 400th ranked candidate will not be eligible for admission to the school.
>
> This will therefore inform parents as to whether to name The Tiffin Girls' School as one of their choices on the Common Application Form, which must be sent to the local authority by 31st October. Only candidates who have been invited to stage 2 testing should name the school as a preference on the CAF.
>
> Stage 2 testing will include three tests which will assess numeracy and literacy: one each of mathematics, reading and writing. These tests will be at an appropriate level of challenge to determine the offer of places at the school and will be guided by the content of the Primary National Curriculum. For guidance only: the level of challenge of these

tests will be appropriate for candidates anticipated to achieve Level 5 at the end of Year 6.

The mark for final ranking will be weighted as follows: 30% Stage 1 test result and 70% Stage 2 test result. Candidates will then be ranked and that ranked score list forwarded to the Local Authority.

Whilst this may all seem confusing, remember that everyone else is in the same boat and the schools themselves do want you to apply, so if in doubt give them a ring or pay them a visit, talk to the admissions secretary or registrar and get them to spell it out to you in detail. Be aware that the most popular and oversubscribed state schools simply cannot handle the sheer number of potential parent enquiries and school visit requests, so largely insist on open days and the use of their websites for information.

Choosing a School

So how do you choose a school? It is clearly somewhat of a minefield, and we have therefore listed some questions below to help you think about what you actually want. We have covered many of these issues in more detail elsewhere in this book. This is not necessarily an exhaustive list, and so, as everyone's circumstances and needs are different, you may well think of other things to consider. As you research the options, visit schools, attend open days and talk to other parents, you will come up with your own questions for those schools as well, so we have left a space for you to jot anything else down.

QUESTIONS TO ASK YOURSELF:

- *Do I want a very academic school?*
  A look at league tables, press reports and 'word on the street' should give you an idea of how academic a school is.
- *Do I want a co-ed school (boys and girls together)?*
  People often like a girls' school for girls and a mixed school for boys. How does that work?
- *Do I have any religious or ethical beliefs that need to be considered?*

How do you feel about a 'Catholic' or 'Christian Science' school? How strongly 'religious' do you want it to be?

- *Do I want a 'traditional' feel to the school or a more relaxed approach?* This is not about better or worse. School culture really does vary, and obvious indicators include the extent to which strict uniform rules are enforced, whether the children stand up when a member of staff comes into the classroom, etc.

- *Do I want a school which excels in a certain area such as sport or music?* What about excellence in science and technology or creative arts? Just because the school has a label of 'specialist science school' does that mean its science teaching is actually any better than another school without that label?

- *Does my child have the ability to be awarded a scholarship?* Scholarships vary considerably in the standard required and the size/form of the reward. They usually want something back in terms of the ongoing commitment required by the child.

- *Does my child require 'special needs' support?* How much will this cost? Which lessons will my child miss for the extra support?

- *If my child is struggling, is there a 'homework/subject clinic'?* What other one-to-one support is available, and are children encouraged to ask for it?

- *What is my view on which languages are taught?* How about Latin and Greek? If you have a particular skill in a modern language and/or family in another part of the world then you will be well placed to help your child with that language and perhaps gain firsthand experience of it.

- *Do I think that sciences should be taught separately for year 7 pupils?* This varies from school to school. Schools also vary in their attitude to separate science GCSEs versus a combined science qualification.

- *Do I want a city school?* A local school? What are the travel options available?

- *What is the surrounding area like?*

When your 13-year-old daughter wants to meet up with her friends you need to know where they can go safely.

- *Are there any hidden costs?*
  For example, will you have to buy a laptop or expensive sports equipment? Will there be a lot of 'compulsory' trips that you will have to fund? How often and to where?
- *For private schools - what about fees, bursaries and assisted places?*
  Not all private schools cost the same as each other.

Space for your own thoughts about your priorities:

QUESTIONS TO ASK THE SCHOOLS:

As well as referring to the questions above, here are some additional questions. How about asking different members of staff the same questions to see if you get consistent answers!

A word of advice: On your first visit do not take your child; if they love it and you really don't, there may be problems. A 9- or 10-year-old does not know enough to make an objective decision and will be unduly swayed by superficial things that will have little or no bearing on their long term happiness in the school.

- *What level should my child be performing at in order to be happy at this school/pass the exam to get into this school?*

- *What is your school ethos?*
  How do you outwork your values?
- *How big are the classes?*
  What is the teacher/pupil ratio?
- *How often are there parent/teacher reviews?*
- *Can I communicate easily with my child's form tutor?*
- *What is the 6th form provision?*
  This is especially important if your child already shows an interest in a particular subject.
- *Do most of the children get their first choices for GCSE?*
- *What provision is there for 'gifted and talented'/learning difficulties?*
- *Which subjects are set?*
  Are the classes streamed? Note that 'streamed' is where a whole class is one ability level and 'sets' is where children move to a top/middle/bottom group for that particular subject.
- *What extra-curricular activities are on offer?*
- *Do most of the activities happen at lunchtime or after school (try to pick up a list)?*
  This may affect the journey home if you are relying on a school bus or public transport in the dark, winter evenings.
- *How often do matches happen on Saturdays?*
  This may be relevant if your child is already in a club as schools expect their matches to take priority. Usually you are asked to take them to school for a bus that will transport them to away matches.
- *How many hours are there of compulsory sport?*
- *Does the school offer 'Duke of Edinburgh'?*
- *Are there any unusual subjects that this school offers, e.g. Mandarin, Astronomy, Child-Development, Electronics, etc.)?*
- *How often do the children actually participate in science experiments?*
- *What is the procedure when a child is disruptive in lessons?*
  How many children have been suspended or excluded from the school in the last twelve months?
- *What happens if my child does not arrive at school?*
  Will someone contact me?

- *Is there an 'end of the day registration'?*
  Does the school know for sure that all pupils are in attendance? Does it have an electronic access system so no pupil can enter or leave without being recorded? Is it fool proof?
- *What would happen if a child is caught smoking?*
- *How does the school deal with bullying?*
  Ask to see records of how bullying is dealt with, which you are entitled to do under the Freedom of Information Act.
- *Is there a 'buddy' system?*
  Where relevant, does this apply to the journey as well?
- *Where do most children go on to?*

OBSERVATIONS TO MAKE ON A SCHOOL VISIT

Aside from the 'hard facts' you can glean from the questions above, when you make a visit to a school it is possible to pick up a certain 'vibe' or sense of the school. You will get better at this the more you do it so do not be afraid of going back for a second or even third visit if they will let you.

Here are some things to keep your eyes open for:

- *Do the children look happy and well-behaved?*
  Try to be around during break time. This can be very informative!
- *What equipment and facilities can you see in use?*
  Be aware that all the best equipment is generally brought out on the 'open day' where a few children have been selected to demonstrate it so always try to visit the school during a normal day as well.
- *Look at displays and the quality of work in exercise books.*
  Ask to see random examples of work and take a look for teachers' comments and marking.
- *What text books do they use?*
  How old are they?
- *Is your 'Tour Guide' the sort of person you would be happy for your child to become?*

Be careful with this one. No two children are the same, and you could just be lucky/unlucky with your allocated guide.

- *Are children attentive in lessons?*
  What are the noise levels like?
- *What happens at the changeover bell?*
  Do you get knocked over, or is a door held open for you?
- *How do the children individualise the school uniform?*
  Keep an eye on use of make-up and jewellery and check what the school rules are to see if they are being enforced!
- *What do the children look like after school?*
  How do they behave?

If you are being given a tour by a guide then try asking them these questions:

- *Do children have set places in registration, or are they allowed to sit on desks (this may be true of older children)?*
- *What happens in form time?*
- *How much homework do you get?*
- *What do you do if you don't understand the work?*
- *How often do you have assemblies, and what are they about?*
  In a Catholic school you may want to ask if everyone goes to mass and how often does it happen?
- *How often do you find equipment broken or not working?*
- *Who is your favourite teacher and why?*
  This could be quite enlightening if they tell you!
- *What would you do if you or your friend were being bullied?*
  Who would you go to see?
- *Does the Headteacher know who you are?*
  Does he/she know everyone? In a small school the answer simply must be "Yes" whereas in a larger school that may be somewhat unrealistic.
- *Is it only the 'best' children who get to play in matches or orchestras?*

Bear in mind that a lot of the questions in the above lists do not necessarily have a right or wrong answer. What you are trying to do is build up a sense of character of the school and the way pupils **and** teachers behave. You want to understand the school's attitude to pastoral care and discipline, and that is not just what they tell you - it is what happens in reality, and that may not be the same thing!

Good leadership in a school is going to make a huge difference, and a poor school with a new, talented head at the helm may actually be a much better place to send your child than a reasonably good school that has been the same for years.

ARTICLE: Discerning Effective Leadership and Management in Schools

By Alison Taylor, Head of HR, Askham Bryan College, York

What with one thing and another, through both my employment experience as an LEA School Adviser and later senior manager of a local FE college, combined with my School Governor and parental experiences, I have had the (mostly!) great pleasure of touring literally scores of different schools. One thing I am convinced about is that a school with great leadership and management will be a successful school. I believe this so passionately that I rejected the 'steady' and 'successful enough' local school for my two elder children back in the 1990's and sent them instead to a school that had recently been declared as being in special measures, and all because I had so much confidence that the newly appointed headteacher there would provide the much needed leadership to make a rapid impact and turn the school around. I did not regret my decision, and my children thrived and excelled with the new head at the helm. But how does great leadership manifest itself, and how can it be discerned in the relatively short time parents spend looking round a prospective school? Here is a short summary of my thoughts which I hope may be helpful to you.

Firstly, the very obvious: any headteacher should exude passion for their school and, when asked about its mission and values, should come alive explaining to you what this means in practice. If there is no energy coming forth when you ask them to share their thoughts on where they would like to see the school go over the next few years, or if the response is distinctly lacklustre, then this may be a cause for concern. If the head is not inspired themselves, then it is more than likely that the staff and learners are similarly uninspired! The response need not necessarily be extravert and gregarious, but even in the quietly determined there should be a clearly thought-through focus about what s/he wants to see achieved in their own school.

Questions you may wish to consider asking on a visit:

- *Could you talk me through the school's vision and values, and how are these embedded into the life of the school?*
- *What do you enjoy most about working at this school?*

Secondly, and leading on from this, is the honesty and openness shown by school leadership teams about where they need to improve. No organisation is perfect, and I've seen very good schools demonstrate ugly complacency. For me, any organisation should admit its weak points and be clear about what it wants to do better and not feign perfection to dupe customers; schools are no exception. LEA schools will have a School Improvement Plan which should outline actions which you may wish to see and talk through with a headteacher, to assess how meaningful the document is and whether you can, in reality, see any of the actions coming to fruition.

Questions you may wish to consider asking on a visit:

- *What are your top three priorities for the school for the short to medium term?*
- *How does the school identify the areas it wants to improve upon and how do you ensure all staff buy into this?*

Thirdly, are the rest of the staff team engaged and ready to deliver an excellent education for your child? Whilst I don't want to advocate a culture of presentee-ism in the office, I do have to say that the first inkling I had that a school local to where I live was underperforming was when I passed it every morning on my way to work just before 8am and no staff cars were in the car park. Ever. Nor were they there whenever I came past even as early as 6pm in the evening. Somehow it told me something: the head clearly couldn't be bothered to put in the hours, so nor could his staff. A year later, and that school has just been deemed unsatisfactory by Ofsted, and the head is making a rapid departure.

I think it is perfectly appropriate to ask a headteacher about how the school motivates and retains its staff, given that when staff leave, particularly mid-year, it can be very disruptive to curriculum delivery. Similarly if the school has a high level of staff turnover, this may be a sign that they are all worthy of promotions that just are not available in that establishment, or it may be indicative of a lack of commitment to the direction the organisation is going in. Whatever the reason, an effective head should be able to provide a depersonalised account of why any unusual numbers of staff may have left recently and how the students' needs were adequately catered for despite the departures.

I always think it is interesting to observe the interaction of the head with other members of staff and also to hear staff talk about the head in private. Anything less than a healthy respect in more than the odd isolated case may well be a cause for concern and worthy of further follow-up.

Questions you may wish to consider asking on a visit:
- *What steps does the school take to motivate and retain high performing staff?*
- *How many staff have left the school over the last year or two?*

I'm sure that, like me, once you've toured several different schools, you'll quickly pick up the culture in each and a strong feel for whether the school is well led and managed, but hope that this article is useful in shaping your thoughts and making sense of your first impressions. Happy school hunting!

How Do You Choose Your Chocolate?

Alison Taylor's article gives you some thoughts on how to assess the school's leadership. But how else can you possibly decide? What does influence your choice of chocolate from the box?

- the look or image;
- the written description;
- the advice of someone else;
- prior knowledge and experience.

Close your eyes and experience the joys... or disgust!

Who do you believe? What do you believe? How about the Good Schools' Guide or maybe Mumsnet? Do you listen to parents at the school gate? Do you look at league tables or websites? Are you swayed by glossy brochures? Be grateful you live in a country where you have some legal protection against false claims and can broadly believe facts that are presented to you by the schools. We came across one expensive boarding school in Uganda where their glossy brochure showed a beautiful swimming pool and stated it was a part of their facilities. When we toured the school and spoke to some of the pupils we found out that no such pool had ever existed!

We have information overload and it is very stressful and ultimately we have too much choice. We stand in the supermarket and are bemused by shelves of cereals – even that can be stressful when each member of the family has a different preference! How much more stressful is it to choose a school that will ultimately shape your child at an impressionable time and affect the person that they are going to become?

Personally I (Anita) would not take too much notice of opinions voiced about specific schools on parents' forums. The views are going to be varied, diverse and ultimately, unreliable. One parent can love a school and another will vilify the same school. Yes, by all means ask other parents practical questions such as, "Which sports do they play?" but even asking questions about how much homework the children get set can be tricky. One child may manage to do all of their homework in 45 minutes but it may take another child 3 hours! I have seen online forum discussions about schools I have taught in and I have read comments by people who do not have anything to do with the school but say they do not like it because they know someone who knows someone who once found a parent at that school to be rude!

It is quite amazing how some parents can be totally desperate to get their child into a particular school and as soon as they fail to do so they seem to be on a mission to denigrate and publicly criticise the school at every opportunity, so be careful who you listen to.

THE GOOD SCHOOLS GUIDE

The Good Schools Guide (GSG) is an independent resource and is particularly useful if you are moving areas. GSG says:

> *We offer a unique and in-depth analysis of approximately 1200 of the best independent schools in the UK. Each review is critical, informative and highly readable, with particular attention being paid to such matters as what kind of school suits each child, and what its pupils and its parents are like. It asks the questions that the prospectuses don't broach in order to highlight the strengths and weaknesses that mere facts can't.*
>
> *In addition, on our website (**www.goodschoolsguide.co.uk**) we analyse all the school information we can get hold of: which universities and courses pupils go on to, subject-by-subject results analysis, catchment area data and much more.*
>
> *We also offer one-to-one consultation with our editors for those with particularly knotty problems to solve.*

It is important that the editors are independent and often parents. The schools do not pay them so they are not biased in any way.

LEAGUE TABLES

Here we hit a potential problem. Take note: league tables are not always correct. They only record results based on certain GCSEs under certain conditions. Critically, they do not register iGCSE's (more advanced GCSE exams) which a lot of the schools now use, and neither do league tables take account of children who take exams a year early. One independent school near us this year had to publish a significant comment on this as its league table positioning had effectively been incorrectly lowered as a result of these omissions.

As a result of this and other reasons the Independent Schools Council (ISC) and its constituent member associations cautions against taking too much notice of league tables. Specifically the ISC says on its website (**www.isc.co.uk**):

> *School league tables can be misleading, particularly for parents who are looking to find the best school for their individual child. Education is about the 'whole' child. School exam results tables do not measure pastoral care, soft skills and many other facets of education which are essential parts of schooling. As a result, ISC does not, and has never published school league tables.*
>
> *Often external parties take the spreadsheet of ISC schools' exam results and construct league tables from the raw data. ISC advises against the creation of any league tables and advises caution in any use or interpretation of them. In the past, mistakes have been made when bodies outside of ISC have attempted to construct league tables. For example, schools with similar names have been omitted and/or UCAS points have been incorrectly calculated.*

INSPECTIONS

Any teacher will tell you that the most stressful part of their lives is usually the time the school is inspected. One disastrous lesson can skew the inspector's report and usually everyone knows who was responsible even if they were not directly singled out. However, inspectors are experienced and know what to look for, and for the most part are very good at correctly assessing the essence of what a school is about, its strengths and weaknesses and how that has changed since the last inspection.

School inspection reports can often be found on school websites but, confusingly, there are multiple inspection organisations. There are 1,250 schools that are members of the Independent Schools Council, and these schools are regularly assessed by teams from the Independent Schools Inspectorate. Private religious schools are separately inspected by the Bridge Schools Inspectorate, and schools not covered by either of these are inspected by OFSTED. In addition, Catholic and Church of England diocesan inspectors will visit the corresponding faith schools on their patch. Unfortunately for parents, these organisations all have differing inspection processes and assessment criteria so it is not always possible to compare apples with apples.

Our recommendation would be to read any and every inspection report you can get a hold of for the schools you are interested in, but try to avoid doing too much of a comparative analysis based on those reports alone, especially if they are not all carried out by the same organisation.

Occasionally inspectors, although well-meaning, do get a little pedantic such as:

- **"Behaviour management", while exemplary, was not explicitly stated in the school policy.**

...or our favourite (you have to laugh!)...

- **Children have "not been taught how to play appropriately" because at break and lunchtimes they "often run around the small area shouting and letting off steam".**

VALUE ADDED

'Value Added' is a term which keeps cropping up, and it is important you understand what it means. All children moving on to secondary education will be baseline assessed as soon as they enter secondary school and will be measured against benchmark standards of national curriculum attainment levels. This is used to predict how well the children will do in the future, and hence a child with a certain set of levels at year 7 will be expected to achieve a given number of GCSE grades in year 11.

'Value Added' is a measure of how well the child achieves in relation to their predicted outcome when they started at the school. The Value Added score is worked out by comparing the predicted grades with the actual grades. This can be seen on some school websites where they may publish a graph demonstrating their Value Added ability. Some schools in our local area are rightly proud that their actual GCSE grades average 20% higher than predicted. Smaller, less academically selective schools in particular often focus on their Value Added capability, priding themselves on getting the best out of the pupils.

As with so many of these school comparisons, be careful. A selective school that only takes very academic pupils will have an intake where the children are predicted a very high number of A and A* grades at GCSE. In practice it is impossible for such a school to significantly over-achieve so it is normal to see a lower Value Added score for highly academic schools.

State versus Private

If ever there were a topic to get educationalists hot under the collar then this is it. Let us be quite clear here. Anita teaches in a state school and our children were in state schools but are now in the private system for very specific reasons due to their skill set and characters. This book is written on the basis that there is a place for both, and even if you do not like the existence of the private system, it is not about to go away. It gives parents an additional set of choices, and you may as well at least understand what it means for you.

Whether you like it or not some statistics speak for themselves. If you go to a private secondary school your chances of getting a good degree from a top university are dramatically higher.

According to the Guardian in March 2011:

- 7% of children are educated in the private sector but 47% of 'Oxbridge' students went to private school;
- 25% of students in Russell Group universities were privately educated;
- A third of all pupils obtaining three A grades at A level are from the private sector.

Many parents are happy to go through the state primary school system but want something different for secondary schools. Unfortunately some of the state secondary schools have had bad press in the news, but in our area we are very fortunate to have thriving state secondary schools which are improving year on year. I, Anita, work very closely with one in particular on a day-to-day basis, and I am glad to be able to teach primary school children who go on to that school.

If you are considering a private school then, as discussed previously, look at the Value Added score. Generally there are more trips and a wider range of learning experiences on offer from private schools. Look at the attitude to learning. Many of the more academic schools have an accelerated learning approach which is why they manage to achieve so many A* results. Will your child cope with this and the resulting constant pressure?

The state system is more mixed ability and takes children from a wide range of backgrounds. It will therefore give your child much more of an impression of 'normal life' and hence, in theory at least, a greater ability to mix with a wider range of people.

DISCIPLINE IS SEEN AS AN ISSUE

In June 2008 the BBC reported that a new Ipsos MORI poll for the Independent Schools Council showed that 57% of parents in the state sector would go private if they could afford to do so. After the rather general sentiment of "wanting a better education", the second most significant reason for wanting to go private was discipline, cited by 30% of parents as a reason for choosing private and, significantly, up from only 14% in 2004. All other major indicators stayed roughly the same.

See **http://news.bbc.co.uk/1/hi/education/7440022.stm** for more details and some interesting comments by readers.

If I (Anita) may be permitted to venture an insider's opinion here, there is probably some validity to these concerns. Having taught in half a dozen state secondary schools I can say with some confidence that it is getting harder for state schools to deal with the most difficult children. Exclusion rates have dropped in recent years – not necessarily because children are better behaved but because it is harder to exclude them, and hence they continue to cause trouble. The independent sector has no problem with this. It simply tells them to leave. Sadly, that does not usually help the difficult child, but it certainly helps all the other children and teachers adversely affected by their behaviour!

PARENTS WANT 'VALUE' AND HAPPY CHILDREN

A friend of mine said private schools are for the 'wonderfully wealthy', 'passionate professionals' or the 'serious sacrificers'. I don't know how you see yourself, but if you are considering paying you need to be sure that the product is good. There are some very average private schools out there as well so be sure you are getting value and, if you do put your child in a private school, remember you are the client and you can continue to hold them to account. If you find out through a report or parents' evening that your child has been struggling in Maths for the last 6 months or has not handed their homework in all term then why are you only now being told about it? You have a right to expect better than that!

Ultimately, of course, it is about finding the right school for the child. Education is not about one size fitting all. One good friend said this to me recently:

> *"Don't assume one system suits all. Don't assume private suits everyone. I have one daughter who is much happier in the state system*

(having been to two different private schools) and one who is happier in the private system."

I know the children concerned and I know this is absolutely true. The parents were quite prepared to pay for the daughter in question but she is thriving in a local comprehensive in a way she consistently failed to do in higher pressure, selective private schools.

PERCEIVED PROS AND CONS

The following is a mixed collection of opinions we have gathered over the years. It is not intended to be either for or against private education per se but instead summarises much of what appears to be the majority view amongst parents that we talk to. Note that some views appear to contradict each other, and we have not attempted to hide this – different people have different opinions, and you will have to make up your own mind too!

- "Smaller class sizes (in the private sector)";
- "Although private schools have smaller class sizes state schools usually have a Teaching Assistant (primary only) and, where necessary, a special needs helper in the classroom";
- "Because my child is reasonably bright and mildly dyslexic he wouldn't have had support within the state sector as he achieves higher than the national average anyway";
- "My daughter who has a SEN Statement has one-to-one help in the local state school";
- "More sport - he's a boy!" (private);
- "The flexible boarding option means that my child can stay at school after playing lots of sport";
- "If you feel that you do not have much money then in the private system you can feel quite poor if you don't have a big house, lots of holidays etc";
- "In a private school you can get your identity through other stuff than academia";
- "In a private school you have to fit a mould and reflect the ethos of the school. My daughter has a unique outlook on

life, and she couldn't express herself within the private system";

- "Better discipline and pupil behaviour within the private sector";

- "There are some small private schools that aren't very good and the teachers aren't qualified teachers but in the state schools at least you know what you're getting";

- "The safeguards are much better in the state system and 'nuisance children' are dealt with";

- "Now my child is older I can see that there is a lot of support for University applications such as Oxbridge" (private);

- "The standard of Music is amazing – my daughter would not have experienced this anywhere else" (private);

- "My daughter believes in herself more within the state system as she can keep up. The school have found her skill set, promoting her self-esteem";

- "There are more educational opportunities available in the private sector, and it offers a broader education";

- "I would rather have free education and pay for clubs and activities outside school";

- "According to the (state) school my daughter was not performing to her potential, she was mildly disruptive and it was unclear why. She started to become withdrawn and disinterested and her relationships were being affected. As a result of being in a large prep school (5 years) she is motivated and has developed her self-esteem as they have developed what she is good at".

In the interest of balance, and to help those who are struggling with the state/private debate, we have included the following article by a parent who has children thriving in both state and independent schools.

ARTICLE: State versus Private – a Parent's Perspective

By an anonymous parent

As a parent, it is always essential to be open minded when trying to find the most suitable schooling for your children, but this is never truer than if you are fortunate enough to be in the position to choose between state or private education. With the luxury of choice comes a baffling array of considerations.

Often it is assumed that those who can afford it 'should' go private as this is the best possible route for their child. For others, because they can afford it, it will be the only route they ever consider, automatically discarding state education as the poorer relative. However, I have learned from my own experience with my own children that it is absolutely vital to look at each of them as an individual and spend time and effort discerning the most appropriate learning pathway for them. Private schooling is not necessarily the most fitting option.

I consider that my own children are lucky because they have been educated at various points in time in both state and private schools. This was not the plan when my oldest child started out in the local primary school but life's circumstances have dictated the need to be flexible, and I feel more enlightened as a result. Over time I have come to realise the benefits that such varied experiences have brought them and I have proceeded to be bolder when considering next moves. Their horizons are broad; they are accepting of all walks of life and they are learning to be content with who they are and what they stand for as individuals, irrespective of their learning environment. It is hard to put a value on such important life skills.

The two sectors' end products are fundamentally different, and clearly because you are paying, the private school package looks - and is - excellent at high end appeal. Most notably, private schools are highly regarded for their small class sizes - and for one of my children this has been brilliant.

She lacked confidence and self-esteem, and in her larger state school class she 'hid' and felt desperately inadequate in the face of her 'brilliant-at-everything' friends. Moving on to a private school where she became one of sixteen has given her the confidence to speak out and she is beginning to feel that what she can offer is of value to her teacher and her peers.

For another of my children those same small class sizes proved to be her undoing. She is an ebullient and confident girl with bags of energy and bubble, irrepressible enthusiasm and drive. In a small class, it was hard to squeeze her into the school mould and to contain her was tricky. She struggled and temporarily lost her identity; her teachers struggled with her and her friends became irritated by her. Moving her at the appropriate time to a huge state high school where she was no longer a big fish in a small sea was exactly what she needed. Here she was able to find her own level, and her wonderful vivaciousness was suitably diluted by the volume of a further twenty nine characters. She loves the dynamic nature of a big learning environment, and it in turn is able to cope with her. As a result she is thriving.

But my son presents another scenario. He is painfully shy and cannot cope with any attention or individual focus; he completely lost his self-confidence in a small prep school class! He lived in fear of being asked a question in class and it was too small for him to find a soul mate. For him, moving him to a state school where he became one of thirty was an incredibly positive decision. What he lost in the individual teacher attention to his studies he gained in a wide choice of friendship groups and the anonymity with which he was free to observe the hustle and bustle around him.

Private schools offer so very much in terms of extra-curricular activities, and for me this is one of their biggest draws. As a busy working parent I know that these activities will occur within the school grounds, either during the school day or after it requiring little input (other than the occasional financing of a paying club) from me. The after school option gives me an extra half an hour in my working day, during which time I am confident that my daughter is happy and safe.

I am grateful that the school have offered her a balance of activities, and she is able to access as many as she wants of them. How fabulous, for example, to watch her thrive in cookery club after school one day, and cross country the next. Her sense of triumph as she wins competitions more than makes up for the fact that she struggles in Maths and English, and sits in the bottom sets for both. Through being given the opportunity to develop as a whole person she is learning to believe in herself and what she can offer life. This is a real gift. She is realising that success in Maths and English, while extremely important, need not be her raison d'être. Previously in her primary school she was one of a large pool of girls and she didn't 'shine' sufficiently in netball, football or cross country to be picked for a team. Thus she deemed herself 'rubbish'.

For me as a parent, it was one of the most compelling reasons for moving her to a private senior school: I desperately wanted her to have the opportunity to have a go. On the other hand, my other daughter who is at a state high school is happy to throw herself into an array of activities that we as parents are able to facilitate, whether or not she is good at them. The shorter school day and less homework means that she has more time to develop extracurricular interests – but she must set out to find them and discover her niche for herself.

When a child has particular educational needs, parental wisdom is of paramount importance. There is a well-founded argument that says that if a child's needs are sufficiently severe to merit a statement and hours of one- to- one support from a Special Needs Assistant, then keep them in a state school. They will be finely catered for here, in an accountable system that follows a recognised structure. However, if as in my case you have a child who slips through the net – is too weak to go through school without a struggle, has a specific diagnosis but is not bad enough to get any extra support, then I have found myself looking towards a private education.

Here I know that the extra attention they will get from a smaller class will help them in a way that remains a distant hope in a big class. They may well be 'understood' better by a teacher who has the luxury of time that their counterpart in a larger class in an underfunded state school just doesn't have – despite all good intentions and desires. Consequently such children often appear to lose their 'naughty' label as they start to re-build their sense of self-worth. I have witnessed this transformation first hand.

So in summary: I would urge all parents faced with choices for the educational future of their children to open their eyes to the individual characteristics and needs of each child. If bank balance allows, please look at both private and state schools. Put aside any prejudices, or unhelpful playground talk, and go and see both types of set-up for yourselves. And then listen and watch. Listen to your child and their feelings. Validate them and trust them, for they know themselves well. Listen to the teachers at the schools you visit. Watch them interact with your children – and watch your children react to them. Watch the pupils in the school you are visiting – will your child fit in? Only by being truly open and alert to your children and their needs and wants can you make the best educational choices for them. It's an exciting, liberating and privileged position to be in. Take your time and enjoy the journey.

Boys, Girls and the Mixed School Debate

We heard somewhere that girls do better in single sex schools and that boys do better in co-ed. Does that mean therefore that the co-ed schools are boy-heavy? We think that some of them are, and that is worth looking into, especially if you have a daughter.

Single sex schools dominate the league tables, so if you are purely looking at exam results you may want to consider them. If you have only sons or only daughters you may want to consider co-ed because they will not be mixing with the opposite sex at home. Don't let one person's experiences (yours!) dominate your thinking too much. I (Anita) went to a girls' school and hated it. Tim went to a boys' school and loved it. Our daughter is at a girls' school and is very glad to be there. Our son loves his mixed school environment and some of his best friends there are girls. You know your children best so try to think about what will work for them.

In the mid teens girls' and boys' brains are very different, which is reflected in how they learn. Boys love competition, but for girls this could undermine their friendships and develop insecurity. Girls need encouragement and boys need to be pushed. There is, however, research by the Department of Children, Schools and Families (2005) that says there was "little evidence to support the notion that the dominant learning style of boys differs from those of girls". There is also contradictory research about whether it is better or worse to be in a co-ed environment in relation to awareness of the opposite sex. There are those who say that the boys mess around in front of the girls for attention, but some say they work better because they want to compete with them. Research also shows that girls in a co-ed school are less obsessed with body image. Ultimately it is still about choosing the right school for your child.

ARTICLE: Benefits of Single Sex Education
By Michael Connolly, Headmaster, Cranmore Preparatory School

Choosing the right school at any stage for your child can be a minefield. There are so many factors to consider from ethos to academic rigour, extra-curricular opportunities to sheer transport logistics that school selection is most definitely not a case of 'one size fits all'.

Boys and girls think differently and develop at different stages, and some children will simply thrive more in a single sex school. Since 1964, a series of studies has confirmed that boys' and girls' brains are organised differently, that the differences are genetic and substantially more significant than those associated with age. The main areas of difference that impact upon brain development and maturity include hearing, play behaviour, reactions to stress, ability to express feelings, behaviour in the classroom and overall approach to learning. Teachers at a single sex school recognise and work with the way that boys and girls learn best and adapt their approach and style to suit the needs, performance and progress of their pupils. For example, specifically "boy-focused" approaches such as appealing themes and characters have significant results for reading and writing progress. Research shows that boys generally have better spatial skills, more acute vision, learn best through touch, are more impulsive, more physically active and competitive and need to be given "hands-on" lessons.

Within a single sex school, both genders can develop emotionally at their own pace with less social pressure and, with boys maturing later than girls, this can foster age-appropriate development that is lacking in the outside world. For both boys and girls, there is the space and environment to just be themselves, not worry about what the opposite sex think of them or how certain subjects are viewed; classification of subjects or activities as for 'nerds' or too 'girlie' is avoided, so girls may be keener to study Maths or boys to study art, music or drama. This advantage is supported by findings which show that boys can be helped to express emotion by involving them in cultural and artistic activities.

In today's society, children are under pressure to 'grow up fast' but many parents find that their son's development from pre-adolescent to full-blown teenager is a sensitive transition. It is vital that each boy can be sufficiently challenged whilst being fully supported, and this can best take place in the top two years of a prep school education. Unusually for children aged 11 - 13, there's the opportunity to enjoy life 'at the top' in tangible ways that include a range of cultural and sporting opportunities and build upon the foundations for senior school life.

Gender-stereotyping in terms of curriculum breadth and subject choice is much less prevalent in a single-sex school and this can have an undoubted effect on future career and life choices. As a final endorsement, a Government-backed review in 2007 recommended that the sexes should be taught differently to maximise results and it highlighted that gender stereotyping was weaker in the single-sex sector.

The above article is the view of the headmaster of a boys' prep school. In the interest of balance the following is from the headmistress of a girls' secondary school. Note also that this subject is tackled from the mixed school perspective in Andrew Gough's article further on in this section.

ARTICLE: What Girls Really Need

By Bridget Williams, Headmistress, Notre Dame Catholic School, Cobham, Surrey

As far as I see it, the purpose of our girls' education, within the classroom and beyond it, is to give them a range of options and a positive self image so that they stretch and challenge themselves and then feel proud of all that they achieve. In addition to their professional aspirations, currently four fifths of women in the UK eventually have children. Sixty percent of UK mothers return to work within six months of having a child – this may be financially driven to some degree but it is one of the facts of life for which we in the teaching profession have to prepare girls under our care.

We know that generally the girls in schools such as mine want demanding careers rather than just jobs, and given that the vast majority of them will choose to have families too, they have a challenging future ahead. If they leave us expecting to be perfect wives, perfect mothers and perfect Chief Executives, we have not prepared them for the reality of this challenging future. We must give them the confidence to achieve their best and feel proud of that, whatever that might be, and to be able to work in partnership with others, making full use of the support available to them and have the self assurance to exercise choice.

I think our job at girls' schools is to prepare our girls as well as we can to cope with the complexities and the challenge of the balancing act they will inevitably face in the future. Our duty is to educate girls with "balanced heads, rather than full ones". We have to educate the girls to learn, with our support, about pacing themselves, about commitment, and about being realistic in their expectations of themselves.

One of the achievements the Girls Schools Association (GSA) is proud of is the establishment and development of the "MyDaughter" website, where we have used our combined expertise to support the parents of girls by offering advice and insight into all aspects of their upbringing and education.

We find that parents these days want their daughters above all to be well balanced and happy. I believe that girls' schools can offer an all-round, high quality education, well suited to meet the demands of modern society in an all-female student environment, recognised as the best educational opportunity for girls. I am proud that our GCSE and A-Level results consistently achieve high pass rates, but for any school education is more than just exam success. We aim to give real preparation for living, through opportunities offered for teamwork and leadership, as well as developing talents and abilities in a wide range of subject areas, including sports, music, drama, art, dance, public speaking and community service, to enhance and develop essential skills useful in your daughters' future personal and professional lives.

Money Matters

If you are considering independent schools then you will need to think about the cost. If you are reading this section despite having no money then keep going as there is hope for you too. If you are a relatively comfortably-off middle class professional with some limited spare cash then you may be in the most difficult situation.

If you are a higher rate tax payer (40%), but not in the 45% band that currently cuts in at £150,000 a year, then to pay £15,000 of school fees (a typical charge for one year) will cost you £25,000 of your income before tax – and we have not included National Insurance in the calculation!

Children are expensive. According to research carried out by Liverpool Victoria Insurance and released in January 2012, it costs a staggering £218,000 to raise a child from birth to 21 and that does not include private education. Private education throughout a child's school life will double that figure.

Broadly speaking, schools recognise this is an issue and do what they can to make their product accessible to a wider range of people. However, ultimately they are semi-commercial organisations that want to attract the best teachers and have the best facilities, and that means charging as much as they can get away with.

Bursaries and Scholarships – More Accessible Than You Might Think

Whatever your circumstances, do not be afraid of asking the school about financial assistance. According to the Independent Schools Council, in 2010/11 around a third of children in private schools received some form of financial help, of which around two thirds of the help given was in the form of means-tested bursaries.

Bursaries are by no means only for the 'really poor'. Whilst it is true that if you are on a consultant surgeon's salary you will not get one, you are certainly potentially eligible if you earn a teacher's wage. The budget schools have for awarding bursaries and/or scholarships varies each year, but school bursars are usually able to give you at least some indication of the number of bursaries or scholarships likely to be awarded. In addition, they will indicate the income levels at which bursaries may kick in, and the school will also know roughly what level of talent they are looking for in order to award a scholarship (such as distinctions at grade 5 music exams for a music scholarship, county level playing for a sports scholarship, etc.)

There are broadly two forms of financial assistance provided by independent schools – bursaries and scholarships. Bursaries are means tested and hence specifically apply to children from relatively less well-off families whereas scholarships are awarded to those who have particularly special academic, musical, sporting or artistic talent regardless of level of 'wealth'.

I (Tim) know of one school that awarded no music scholarships at all one year as they were not that impressed with the ability of any of the applicants. They ring-fenced the money and used it the following year to offer more music scholarships than usual. The budget for scholarships and bursaries is usually exactly that – a budget. So a single 50% scholarship or bursary one year might be replaced by two worth 25% or five worth 10% the next. The lesson in all this is simple: do not assume that you can predict what will be offered this year by what was offered last year as the needs and circumstances of applicants vary every year.

Although scholarships and bursary amounts vary considerably from school to school and from year to year, as a rough rule of thumb they typically range from ten to fifty percent of fees. However, one hundred percent bursaries are by no means unusual, and some schools like to offer them to those from poorer backgrounds to show how generous they can be! Most schools treat scholarships and bursaries entirely independently of each other and hence it is quite possible that a talented child from a less well-off background may be offered a scholarship and a bursary.

DON'T SAY A WORD!

Bursaries are typically kept 'secret', with the absolute minimum number of staff knowing who has been awarded them. This is to ensure children with bursaries are treated no differently by either staff or other pupils. One secondary school bursar told me how bursaries are a nightmare for schools as they can so easily cause all sorts of problems. He told me a story involving one child who had been given a bursary and at some point during the child's life in the school had been on a nice two-week safari to Africa. Another parent, who knew about the bursary, came in to see him, complaining bitterly that they could not afford a holiday this year and just about managed to scrape together the necessary fees, so why did this other family get financial support and then spend the equivalent of a term's worth of fees on a holiday?

On the surface this appears a valid concern. However, the truth is that everyone's financial circumstances are different. The holiday mentioned above could have been a gift from a generous friend or relative who knew that this family was struggling and needed a break. It could have been a competition prize. Or they could have saved rigorously for ten years with the intention of taking their children on one life-changing holiday when they hit a certain age and have already declared those savings to the bursar. For exactly these reasons the bursar in this story now specifically requests that parents who are offered bursaries make a point of keeping very quiet about it and if possible not even telling their children.

The article below is by a parent who has managed to obtain bursaries for his children. It gives you some considerable insight into the process and the issues it sometimes raises.

ARTICLE: Almighty Bursar from whom No Secrets Are Hidden

By 'John Smith', a cash-constrained parent

Bursaries are not just handed out if you ask nicely. You need to demonstrate that you are deserving, and in simple terms that means showing that you do not have enough income to be able to pay the full whack! I did this twice and succeeded both times (for different schools). My financial situation was complex and that made it harder.

My problem was that my income was very erratic. I had multiple concurrent small salaried jobs and was also self-employed. On top of that I did some work through my own limited company. Income levels each year varied a lot and, at the time of applying for bursaries, my main sources of income had dried up and things were tight. All schools require you to fill in a complex form that asks you to declare your household income on a calendar year basis. I did everything on a tax year basis so the calendar year was difficult. You also have to fill in outgoings, mortgage, outstanding loans, number of dependents and all manner of related information. It was hard work pulling it all together, but in the end what I did in both cases was to base it on tax return information and use that as the supporting collateral with a covering letter explaining how I simply could not fill in the form on a calendar year basis.

To be fair to both schools they did actually accept this, and by and large if you declare it on your tax return then they will accept it as fact. They work on the assumption that you are not going to defraud the tax man! Like us, you should expect a home visit and a reasonably thorough grilling from the bursar. If you have nothing to hide then it should not be a problem, and schools do allow you to have a 'reasonable' house and cars as necessary. However, don't expect to get a bursary if you and your two children live in an eight bedroom footballer's mansion with a collection of classic Ferraris unless you can prove beyond doubt that the house and cars belong to someone else and you are simply looking after them! Obviously there are limits to what a bursar can see. Sadly, people do hide the new Mercedes around the corner sometimes, and I am sure a degree of dishonesty exists, but it is the bursar's job to try and suss out the reality behind the numbers.

You will have to keep the school appraised of your financial circumstance every year. You will also have to be careful about how you spend your money. I have a friend who was awarded a bursary at a prep school and was told that it was on the expectation that she was not going to go and buy an expensive car or have an exotic holiday. That sounds tough and rather draconian, but these schools are often charitable trusts that have a legal obligation to do all they can to ensure the money is correctly spent.

Part way through my first child's bursary I was awarded a new contract on a substantial salary. As a result I started earning well. The contract was only for 9 months, but that took me into the window for applying for the second child at a different school.

Two things happened. Firstly, the older child was on an 'assisted place' award which flexes up and down each year depending on declared income so when I declared the next year's tax return that support was lost. Secondly, I simply told the truth to the new school for the second child. I gave them a detailed history and pointed out that whilst I was earning OK right now it was very short term and the last few years my income had been low.

I actually got a very intelligent and fair response. The bursar awarded us a substantial bursary and said, "The only thing I ask is that while you are earning well you don't spend it all. If you lose the contract I don't expect you to immediately come asking for assistance in paying the next year's fees." So my suggestion is be honest. Be completely open. They do have to have formal assessment criteria and they do need to have some structure around the process, but there is more flexibility than you might think.

As a footnote to this story my contract was extended and then eventually cancelled last year. I have checked with one school's finance department, and they have confirmed the assisted place will kick back in again as soon as I send them the new tax return showing the drop in income. It is interesting to note that this school recently wrote to all of the parents asking us to finance a two day residential trip for the children at a cost of £135. We wrote back and said we wanted our child to go but simply could not afford it at the moment and explained why. We had a lovely email reply telling us that the head had been made aware of this and wanted our child to go anyway with a request that if I got a new job would I please try and pay some of it if possible. What a lovely response showing a human touch and a real, pragmatic understanding of difficulties parents sometimes have. As I have already said, honesty will get you a long way.

Dare to ask! You never know what will come of it. Now go and dig out all those payslips.

John's article talks about an 'assisted place'. The fixed bursary is essentially the same percentage discount every year, and the expectation is that you will continue to receive it unless your circumstances change dramatically – such as winning the lottery. An assisted place is a very different beast. It recognises your circumstances at the time of applying but flexes up and down year on year depending on declared income. The good news is that often these assisted places will flex right up to 100% if circumstances demand it, such as a major illness or loss of job, but drop to zero if household income rises dramatically.

SCHOLARSHIPS

The other main way of paying reduced fees is of course by your child being awarded a scholarship. The following is from 'Sue', a parent with a talented child who succeeded in winning a substantial music scholarship.

ARTICLE: Once a Scholar Always a Scholar
By 'Sue Deunim', a parent with a musical daughter

Here's a question for you: why should the child of a premier league footballer earning ten million pounds a year be offered a thirty percent discount on fees just because the child is ultra talented at sport? The discount will make no difference to the family, but another family with less money would value it greatly. I don't know the answer to that, but the point about scholarships is, and always has been, that they are offered regardless of financial circumstances. Part of the reason for this is that scholarships are awarded for the school's benefit as much as the child's. The school wants talented musicians in its orchestras and bands, and part of the deal is that a music scholar continues to have intensive involvement in the musical life of the school so, unlike bursaries, scholarships are very public awards. Sports scholars are required to represent the school at sporting fixtures, and academic scholars are expected to assist with extracurricular science projects, creative writing competitions or whatever opportunities the relevant department head may find. If a child fails to fulfil their scholarly duties then the scholarship may be rescinded.

I spotted early on that my daughter was really musical so I started thinking ahead. I asked around to see what instruments children were learning. I tried her on the violin and that didn't work so, when I realised that schools were often short of oboe players, I found a local teacher and got that moving. My daughter was already a really good recorder player so she found the transition relatively easy. We entered her for exams and worked out what level she needed to get to in order to stand a chance of a scholarship. In general, for creative arts or sports scholarships, the department head will shortlist candidates based on established criteria such as music exam marks, involvement in clubs or orchestras and similar established indicators of prowess so we made sure she joined such groups. Needless to say, she did get the scholarship.

The shortlisted child will be invited to demonstrate their skills by way of an interview and audition of some kind. The Sports, Art or Music head will then make recommendations to the headteacher and, I am given to understand, this is not necessarily a yes/no situation. I believe that if a child is, for example, a simply outstanding violinist and the school is short of good violins then the head of Music may tell the headteacher they want that child at all costs or some such similar sentiment. Clearly every school is different, but I know for a fact that children with scholarships in the same year group in the same school are not always offered the same amount of discount and it is nothing to do with income means testing.

My daughter is required to maintain a heavy involvement in the musical life of the school. At last count she was in chamber choir, main choir, wind band, symphony orchestra and chamber group. Then there's D of E, sports clubs, the annual drama production and the inter-form dance competition. She loves it! She loves school. What more could I want? (Stop Press: As of 2014 she is now section leader in her County Youth Orchestra, does annual music tours to interesting parts of the world and has been offered places to study Music at 5 top universities.)

Academic scholarships tend to be assessed somewhat differently to music or sports awards. Some schools set extra exams for specific subjects, and hence someone may apply for a Maths scholarship and sit an additional, particularly taxing Maths exam. Some schools simply offer academic scholarships to those who got the highest marks in the entrance exams.

As with bursaries, scholarships usually range from ten to fifty percent. Some schools remain very flexible about what scholarships they offer each year whilst others are intransigently restrictive, insisting they will offer "two academic scholarships each worth twenty percent of fees". However, twenty percent is not always twenty percent! One parent I know found that a school that offered a larger music scholarship was actually a poorer financial deal because it did not include free lessons. The school that offered a smaller fee discount also gave the child in question free music lessons worth £200 a term, i.e. another five percent of the school fees.

A CALL TO ACTION

If you are serious about scholarships then act right now! Enrol your child into a well-respected club or society for their chosen skill and make sure they do a lot of it. Create a portfolio of achievements – certificates, photographs of them in action, tickets to professional events (concerts, tournaments, festivals) to show the child is interested, etc. Enter them into regional competitions and talent shows. It doesn't matter if they don't win – you don't need to declare the results unless they are amazing. Just an extensive list of documented activity would be enough for most schools to see that you are serious about your child's talent and the main thing a school wants to see behind a talented child is a supportive parent!

Be strategic and clever. If music is their talent then find out what instruments the schools are short of and immediately start your child on that instrument with a teacher who has a reputation for getting quick results. If, as with our son's school, the main team sport is hockey then, if you want to apply for a sports scholarship, concentrate on that rather than rugby!

DEMONSTRATE POTENTIAL

Remember that scholarships are not always about absolute standard, but instead the schools look for potential. So a child that has been playing the violin for six years and has passed their grade five exam will be less highly regarded than a child who has a merit in grade three and only picked it up a year ago. The same applies to athletics, hockey, gymnastics and many other disciplines. If you think that this sounds like pushy parent syndrome then you may be right. This, unfortunately, is how the game is played, and if your child is genuinely talented then they'll largely take it in their stride and gain self-esteem from achieving.

Bursaries and scholarships are not for everyone. Some families have enough money and their children have no single established special talent. However, if in doubt then ask. If you have a year or more before scholarship applications have to be submitted then you might just have long enough to get your child up to a suitable standard.

If you are not sure if you would qualify for a bursary then write a one page summary of your financial situation including outgoings and number of dependants. Although it gives them more work, bursars like this sort of dialogue because above all else they want to offer bursaries to families they believe they can trust to give them open and accurate financial information. In summary, gaining a bursary or scholarship requires work on your part and, in the case of a scholarship, the child's part too. By and large, once they are awarded they stay in place until the end of GCSEs although sometimes bursaries or assisted places run through until end of sixth form. If you can obtain one legitimately it will save you a lot of money.

What is the 11+ and Why 11+?

Comprehensive schools that do not select pupils on the basis of academic ability or aptitude were introduced in Telford in 1965, and now they account for the secondary education of approximately 90% of children in the UK. Before that point all children used to take the 11+ exam in a primary school to determine whether they would go on to the more 'academic' grammar school or more 'practical' secondary modern. Today it refers to any of three things:

1. In areas of the country where the grammar system still exists in one form or another the 11+ is still used as the 'selective entrance exam' to a selective **state secondary**

school and is usually taken at the secondary school and only by children who have specifically applied to do so;

2.   The 11+ is also a term that applies to the exam process used by **independent selective schools** when selecting children applying in year 6 for year 7 entry;

3.   Finally, at the risk of confusing things further, the same term also applies to the pre-test taken by year 6 children looking to start at an **independent secondary school** in year 9 through the 13+ Common Entrance process.

The school websites or the admissions secretary/registrar will be able to answer specific questions pertaining to the nature of the tests, but we have included 2012 criteria in the School's Directory in the regional versions of this book. Some schools also have examples of exam questions on their websites. They all advise, however, against over-tutoring as your child will need to keep up once at the school. You don't want to be paying for private education and tutoring as well so that they can keep up.

The Elevate Eleven website (**www.ElevateEleven.com**) includes details of tutoring and mock-exams in the Esher area. **www.Elevenplusexams.co.uk** lists mock tests in other areas as well.

Finding a Good Tutor

We are entering into pushy-parent dinner party conversation here as everyone has their own opinions on what approach works best but in general:

- A tutor should help your child with exam technique;
- A tutor should recommend appropriate materials;
- A tutor should be able to tell you how your child is achieving and the likelihood of getting into specific schools;
- A tutor should recognise and diffuse pressure put on the child by school/parents.

There are many different styles of tutoring and good and bad points about each. Whichever method you choose or whether you do it yourself you need to know that tutoring does make a difference.

You need to familiarise your child with the different techniques and through practice they will gain confidence. This is essential as otherwise they may have to spend several minutes reading an exam question and puzzling about the approach that they will need to take.

BIG CLASSES

First, there is the 'lots of children' in a hall style (can be 30 children at a time). The plus side of this method is that your child will be in a very competitive environment and will know how well they are doing in comparison with the other children. However, how much individual attention are they getting and are you paying for children just to practise papers or are they taught the techniques? Is there a sign-in or sign-out procedure? Once, our daughter was left outside such a hall sitting in the dark as Anita's car had broken down and there was no-one available to answer a phone in the lesson. She was not an individual. She was merely a statistic and as a result Anita has developed her own somewhat different approach to tutoring (see *Small Groups* below).

INDIVIDUAL TUTORING

The second option that some people like is individual tutoring. You should be paying for quality attention. Is the tutor eating her dinner/on the phone? Is he/she CRB checked? Only one parent has ever asked Anita that! Perhaps that is because they know she is a school teacher, therefore CRB checked, but parents, please do not be embarrassed to ask. Make sure that the tutor also knows the schools in your area and can recommend the best for your child. Once they are practising timed papers, what does the tutor do? Working alone in a strange house on timed papers at the age of 10 can be quite intimidating.

SMALL GROUPS

A third approach is the method I (Anita) prefer for tutoring and that is small groups. The children have the competitive nature of working together but the tutor can help them individually as well. They get to know each other, and I get to know each of them. I don't make them share their scores out loud if they don't want to as some children can be quite sensitive about this. This approach also gives me a chance to spot the strengths and weaknesses of individual children and advise parents accordingly.

The Testing Process

As we stated in our introduction, schools vary in the types of tests they set, but they generally test some combination of Maths, English, verbal or non-verbal reasoning.

Maths and English tests are fairly well understood. Note that in our area schools are placing an ever increasing emphasis on Maths and English. If you are new to all this then you may be wondering what this 'reasoning' stuff is. They fall under the broad heading of Psychometric Tests. Think of them as a little like CAT or IQ tests that you may have done at school. They test the way a child's mind works, exploring their skill with words, numbers and logic.

Verbal reasoning tests specifically explore a child's ability with words and numbers and their skill in spotting various patterns in combinations. Solving an anagram is a form of verbal reasoning. You will find details of all the key types of verbal reasoning question later on in this book.

Non-verbal reasoning is, as you might expect, based on something other than words. The tests involve the child identifying relationships between sequences of diagrams as well as spotting rotation or symmetry of patterns, solving diagrammatic codes and other pictorial logic problems. Again, you will find details of all the key types of non-verbal reasoning question later on in this book.

Children can enjoy doing them once they understand what is required because they are little challenges or puzzles. Be aware that even the brightest children usually need some practice at them because they will otherwise spend half their time in the test figuring out what they are supposed to do. This is why tutoring and plenty of practice is so important.

Please note: Your child will <u>not</u> need to do verbal or non-verbal reasoning if applying for a state comprehensive.

Exam providers

There are two main exam providers in the UK: Granada Learning (known as GL Assessment) and the Centre for Evaluation and Monitoring (CEM), part of the University of Durham. In addition, some schools use Moray House, based in the school of Education at Edinburgh University.

GL is still the choice administrator for most UK Local Education Authorities. They commission their papers from NFER (National Foundation for Educational Research) who formally changed their name to GL Assessment in 2007.

GL have a bank of 12,000 questions which are constantly being revised or changed so that they can provide papers with questions that are not easily predicted. They also develop customised tests for education authorities who want this and can provide bespoke tests for schools.

A County Example of the 11+ Exam

There are different exam providers according to the county where you live. We live in Surrey which is partly state grammar-school based. There are grammar schools in Kingston upon Thames and Sutton. Currently in Surrey the exams are set by the schools themselves using the GL format. The grammar schools in these areas are in great demand. It is impossible for most Surrey children to travel to the few grammar schools that exist so the schools are becoming much tougher on distance travelled (preferring children that live locally) and as I write this the admissions policy at one of the schools is under consultation and hence may change further. Because there are so few grammar schools they are fiercely competitive and only 1 in 10 children that apply are offered places in those schools. The exams are particularly difficult, but if your child practises the CGP books and papers as well, which are harder than the GL papers, they should not have any nasty surprises. Currently the exams at Tiffin School in Kingston are easier than the CGP papers – at least that's what my pupils tell me!

Update as of November 2014: Our local grammar schools have just announced that they may no longer be testing reasoning at all, saying the use of it is 'under consultation' so the rule here is do not assume that because it was one way last year it will necessarily be the same this year.

Moray House

Moray House Tests are used by some schools. They *"provide a useful complement to assessments based solely on attainment and may be used to establish a baseline against which to establish subsequent performance"* (Moray House). For example, the SW Herts Consortium schools, such as the Watford Grammar schools, use them. Parmiter's School describes them as most similar to Bond and has an example to download on their website. Hodder Education produce books based on this type of assessment. It should be noted that, while the style of the questions is not that different to Bond or GL, the way in which Moray House questions are presented is slightly different, usually with little in the way of direct explanation of the question type, instead simply giving a specific instruction such as 'find the missing word'. For this reason practice and familiarisation with different question types is arguably even more important than with other test authorities.

Which Type of Exam should we Expect?

Where schools set their own tests (particularly the independent schools) they may offer an example paper on the website or sometimes send them out to pupils after they have registered. I have recently seen one, from a highly prestigious independent school, that looks completely different from any papers that I have ever seen in the shops! The schools are trying to stay one step ahead of the tutors to ensure that they don't have pupils who are excessively tutored and will not be able to keep up with the work once they are at school. It may therefore be a good idea to expose your child to a variety of materials so they won't be thrown if the exam is somewhat different.

For an up-to-date list of which areas are covered by which exam provider, go to the CGP website. It has a list of which providers are used and can also point you towards the appropriate materials, whether it is GL, CEM or Moray House. Their practice material is of an excellent standard and is used in many schools.

Elevenplusexams.co.uk also has this information and is now selling CEM materials, as are Amazon and larger bookstores.

CEM in More Detail

In recent years CEM (Centre for Evaluation and Monitoring), part of the University of Durham, has become the exam provider for an increasing number of counties. Berkshire, Buckinghamshire, Redbridge, Bexley, Birmingham, Henrietta Barnett and Latymer schools all use CEM questions. This type of questioning is supposed to reflect modern research into the nature of ability and that ability is multi-faceted. CEM questions claim to test a wider range of skills and they are meant to be more 'tutor-proof', although whether this is actually true remains to be seen. This idea behind the CEM testing is to 'reduce any disadvantage between children who are tutored and those who are not' but many children still choose to be tutored or practise materials at home, with wise parents understanding that familiarity, training in time management and widening vocabulary will always give them an advantage over untutored or unpractised pupils. Repeated practice also makes children less anxious in an exam situation. Rather than worrying about the question they proceed from one question to the next, having the prerequisite strategies for tackling the questions.

The CEM exams are more similar to the SATs papers that they do at school, with larger print, simpler layout, etc. Note that children need to have excellent vocabulary and very good spelling. Sometimes the spelling exercises are NOT multiple choice, with the pupils instead having to fill missing letters in boxes.

Importantly, under the CEM system pupils are given a familiarisation document with sample tests to do. They are provided by the schools with examples of questions. The children are also given two practice papers which are set on the same day (or the day before) the exam. There are no commercially available practice papers published by CEM themselves, unlike GL's own papers which are readily available from most good book shops. This is supposed to reduce stress with this approach taking a couple of days rather than the GL 'tutored' approach which for some children goes on for a couple of years! However, Bond and CGP both now offer 'CEM Practice Tests' so tutoring and 11+ preparation is, inevitably, alive and well in the CEM areas of the country.

The idea behind the familiarisation materials is to give the pupils the necessary information without having to be tutored. It shows them how to fill in the multiple choice answer sheet and the format of the test and gives examples of all of the types of questions and the exam procedure. It introduces some of the symbols and phrases used in the assessment.

CEM exams are also multiple-choice and, like GL, the answers will be machine read. Some authorities have a different weighting of each section and with both systems the scores are standardised. Scoring may be different according to the authority and it can be difficult to gauge the total mark or the pass mark. However, some authorities will let the pupils know if there is a particular pass mark (for example, 121 standardised score currently in Buckinghamshire and 111 in Berkshire). The exam is always highly pressurised with short, timed sections that you cannot return to. Most children do not complete all questions so they must start with those that they can do quickly and easily. For this reason the CEM papers tend to have shorter passages for the comprehensions than their GL counterparts. They also include a 'Cloze' type question where blanks need to be filled. There are books available for 'Cloze' type questions through **Elevenplusexams.co.uk**, Amazon etc. Our observation of the CEM-style papers that have been published is that many of them are exactly the same as non-CEM questions but presented in a different format.

Chris Pearse, with whom we co-teach at a tuition centre in Surrey, has written the article below. He has co-authored the '11+ Explained Series', published by GL Assessment, and has experienced CEM testing first hand with tuition centres in Berkshire and Buckinghamshire. We have asked Chris, who is also Managing Director of **www.teachitright.com**, to explain his experience of CEM testing.

ARTICLE: New CEM 11+ System: For the better!

By Chris Pearse, Managing Director, Teachitright

This article provides an overview of the Centre for Evaluation and Monitoring (CEM) which is the new provider for the 11+ exam in certain counties such as Berkshire and Buckinghamshire, where I tutor. Note that some other areas also use this system and the use of it grows every year. You should therefore check with your target schools to find out which system they use.

I have now experienced both GL and CEM providers and definitely believe that the change to CEM is for the better. The testing process is more rigid and involves less 'guesswork.' The Maths and English are more child-friendly, with large text, and are more similar in question-type and layout to the SATs that they do at school. The CEM tests a wider spectrum of skills and supports their school literacy and numeracy work, being more closely related to the school curriculum than the GL counterpart. The children are pleased to make this link with school work, rather than feeling that it is all new and a bit different. This way the 11+ learning process is homogeneous rather than being a separate bolt-on experience.

The CEM 11 Plus is in most cases made up of two tests, each are 45 minutes in length and involve non-verbal reasoning (abstract) and verbal reasoning, and also English and numerical reasoning (maths).

*The **verbal reasoning (VR)** section requires a particularly strong vocabulary, more so than the GL system, and incorporates a variety of word-related questions. For example, odd one out, closest in meaning, opposites, reshuffled sentences and multiple meaning question types are included. Reading is obviously a vital component of having a rich word knowledge and children can also enhance their vocabulary by playing different word games like Scrabble, Boggle and Bananagrams. These games are engaging and can help every child boost their word bank, along with lots of* *reading of course! Throughout the preparation period, using flashcards and word lists repeatedly can help children retain words and develop definitions of high frequency words.*

*The **non-verbal reasoning (NVR)** sections of the paper aim to assess the pupils' knowledge of rotating shapes and recognising patterns. The CEM system has introduced 3D-style questions which involve children answering composite questions, 3D views, 3D plans and analysing nets and cubes. It also includes more common question types such as matrices (grids), lattices (like matrices but set out as a hexagon so relationships need to be found in all directions), sequences, odd one out, finding the figure like the other two or three, and analogies (relationships between 2 figures). Like the verbal reasoning elements of the exam there are many additional activities which can help students gain the specific skills required to do well with NVR such as jigsaw puzzles, model making kits, construction kits such as Meccano and Lego and games such as 'spot the difference' or Sudoku. Developing an understanding of symmetry by drawing shapes onto paper and asking your child to draw in the mirror image can all support non-verbal development. These tasks help children to develop their creativity and ability to solve problems, as well as gaining a better understanding of the world around them.*

*In the **English** part of the tests there are comprehension exercises, cloze tests (words removed from a sentence) and a more concise and detailed comprehension which may include 'filling in the blanks'. The children must ensure they have practised comprehensions for different genres (fiction, non-fiction of various types). Text marking (underlining key points, etc.) is an important skill to develop, that will help children identify the keywords, phrases and statistical information. Often reading the questions prior to looking at the text can also provide a better indication of what to remember while reading the passage.*

***Numerical reasoning** is another important area of the CEM exam system. The questions test mental arithmetic,* *pattern recognition and problem solving. Students also need to have an excellent knowledge of all four arithmetic operations. Jottings can be used on the question paper to help achieve the correct answer.*

The CEM system is designed to test time management. Each section can be quite time pressurised and often children do not finish all the questions before the end of each section. Generally the papers have more questions in each section than they are expected to answer. Also, they are not allowed to return to the section once completed, which could create stress for some children if they are not expecting this. It is important that your child has practised under timed conditions and they must understand that moving on to the next question in order to gain additional marks is preferable to wasting time on one question. When a child feels confident with each question type, and they know the taught strategy and technique, they can use a stopwatch or their own watch to help time themselves. Setting realistic goals for each exercise can help improve their overall time management.

We have been able to develop more 'fun' ways to help the children learn the skills necessary to tackle CEM questions. There are '3D' questions in the nonverbal papers so we practise these in a kinaesthetic way by building 3D towers. We enjoy competitions based on 'Joggle' where the children have to work in teams to put their marbles in a correct order, or Q-bitz which is about creating patterns with cubes.

However, the learning of vocabulary could potentially be arduous, especially with the greater emphasis on words with the CEM exam. To tackle this, we have developed a game and competition-based approach to tutoring which means that the children have the possibility of finding enjoyment even with the most onerous of learning tasks.

This new CEM system has created some anxiety in the 11+ market but the feeling amongst professionals, parents and students is that CEM is trying to make a better link between the national curriculum and the 11+ exam. However, as with other established testing systems, practice and familiarity are key factors for success and by teaching the main strategies and techniques for this exam the children will build up greater confidence. In that respect preparation for CEM or GL-type assessments is exactly the same and bright, well-prepared children will get the places they deserve.

Computerised Testing

Some schools are now introducing computerised testing whereby the children take their entrance exams on computers. The computer programs are very clever. You only have 30 seconds per question (same as on the papers) but you can't go back to any that you have left out. If you have got a certain amount right in a given period of time then the computer takes you on to the next level but the child does not know the level has been stepped up. It would be great for our boys if you could take these on their games consoles! They would achieve such high scores!

This form of testing is supposed to level the playing field and make it fairer on those who have had less practice. The problem is that some of the prep schools have been helping their children prepare for these tests too and, despite the best efforts of the test developers, state school children are still disadvantaged.

Studies have been conducted that demonstrate that paperwork is limiting in terms of item difficulties. Few questions are very difficult and few questions are very easy. A low ability child can find it damaging to their self-esteem if they cannot complete the majority of the paper and conversely the gifted child will not be challenged. The way the computerised, adaptive testing works is so that the children are presented with a higher number of items that are appropriate to their ability.

Source: Identifying Reading Problems with Computer-Adaptive Assessments, C Merrell & P Tymms, Journal of Assisted Learning 23, 2007 Blackwell Publishing Ltd.

There is Another Way

If you are concerned about the competitive nature of the 11+ and have already selected your school then if there is a junior department you may want to enrol your child into one of the earlier years. Many schools let all of the children who are in the junior department automatically go through to the senior department without a further exam, although as a result your child will probably have some form of assessment to enter the junior school. In general this route is probably going to be less competitive, but you may have to pay for an additional few years of education, so if money is not an issue then you could consider this.

Unusually, some children may not get into any of the secondary schools that they have chosen. If the parents really prefer independent schooling then even if all secondary choices have been discounted a child may be able to get into a prep school at age 11 for two years. In Surrey the attitude of the prep schools varies. Some are happy to take children at this age, but many are not as schools of this type tend to discourage pupils from leaving at 11. Hence there are limited new places available in year 7 at these schools.

Another advantage of moving schools at this age could be that you do not feel that your child is ready to move on to secondary education and still needs to be in a more nurturing environment. Being in the top end of a prep school usually coincides with the onset of puberty, and some people feel that this is of significant benefit, effectively allowing children to stay children slightly longer in a 'primary' environment. Many of these children are slower to engage in the teenage socialising and the independence that is accelerated through being in a secondary school.

SPECIAL NEEDS

If your child is not achieving well in the mid-junior age they may have an undiscovered learning difficulty. We discovered that our son was dyslexic at this age so at the start of year 5 we moved him to a school where he could have support with this. Two years later, against all predictions from his original school, he won a place in a selective grammar school where he still gets support when needed.

20% of children have special needs at some point during their school life; sometimes it is obvious, sometimes it isn't. One Christmas when our son was about 8 he tried to tell me that a little boy playing in the playroom wanted his dad. He could not find the word 'dad' and replaced it with the word 'adult'. I started noticing that he began replacing very common words for more complex words and descriptions. I felt that this was unusual but not sure if anything was actually wrong so we paid for an assessment for him. That's when we discovered his dyslexia. Your child may be dyslexic and go on undiagnosed to Oxford or Cambridge, but it is more usual that their coping strategies will limit them at some point throughout their schooling and they will need further input.

According to the Good School's Guide if you recognise more than two or three of the following symptoms in your child to a significant extent then it may be time to think about enlisting some extra help or having them formally assessed by an educational psychologist.

- A lack of pleasure in (or avoidance of) reading.
- Problems with writing, messy presentation, indecipherable paintings.
- Clumsiness - bumping into things, poor spatial awareness and perhaps an inability to hop or to jump properly.
- Not enjoying school.
- Disorganisation - late settling to work, last to pack-up.
- Being easily distracted.
- Generating distraction.
- Reluctance to do homework.
- Not getting on with other children - perhaps avoiding social contact altogether.
- Not thriving at school.

We asked Marlene Caplan, Consultant Psychologist at the Helen Arkell Dyslexia Centre in Farnham, to address these issues for you from her highly experienced, specialist viewpoint and her excellent article is below. Whilst she concentrates largely on dyslexia, much of what she says applies to other special educational needs conditions as well and the bibliography at the end of her article will be helpful to those requiring further reading.

ARTICLE: Learning Difficulties and School Selection
By Marlene Caplan, CPsychol, PhD, Chartered Educational Psychologist, Helen Arkell Dyslexia Centre

Of all learning difficulties, dyslexia is the most common. Estimates indicate that approximately 9% of the population are affected (2% severely). While definitions vary, dyslexia interferes with the development of literacy skills (and associated cognitive processes) often leading to academic underachievement and decreased motivation and self-confidence. Independent of IQ, it has a neurological basis, and occurs more often among boys than girls, although recent research suggests this may reflect the fact that boys are more likely to be referred for assessment.

As transition to secondary school approaches, the presence of dyslexia can pose questions for parents as they begin selecting a school. How can I find the best school to support my child, capitalise on his strengths, and enable him to achieve his potential? What options are there? Where do I begin? What if I suspect that my child has a learning difficulty not yet diagnosed?

What are the indicators of dyslexia?
Dyslexia takes various forms and occurs in varying degrees along a continuum. Depending on the nature and severity, it may come to attention early and be formally diagnosed; in other cases, it may not be identified until much later, if at all. Some children initially appear to progress fairly well, but as school demands increase, parents may notice their child not

keeping pace with classmates, that the transition from 'learning to read' to 'reading to learn' has not transpired fluidly, that spelling and punctuation errors, often an inherent part of early writing skills, have not been rectified. Parents may observe an increasing disparity between what their child seems capable of and school performance. There may be ongoing, subtle signs of problems with information retention, sequencing, word retrieval, and organisation. Homework may become a major battleground. Behavioural issues may surface. For some, despite early intervention, reading may remain slow and effortful, lacking the automaticity required for later school demands. The following checklist may be useful in highlighting dyslexic-type difficulties.

Dyslexia Checklist for Secondary Learners

(Helen Arkell Dyslexia Centre)

READING

- *inaccuracies, including substituting high frequency words*
- *slower speed*
- *difficulty in getting the main idea*
- *problems scanning text for information*

WRITING

- *persistent spelling difficulties*
- *difficulty organising written work*
- *use of simple vocabulary and sentence structure*
- *trouble spotting errors when proofreading*

LISTENING

- *difficulties processing oral information at speed*
- *problems with listening and note-taking at same time*
- *concentration difficulties*

LANGUAGE

- *discrepancy between oral and written skills*
- *word retrieval problems*
- *difficulty with acquisition of topic words*
- *slow to answer oral questions*
- *difficulty with pronunciation of longer words*

ORGANISATION
- *poor organisational and timekeeping skills*

GENERAL
- *difficulties with memory, especially for rote learning*
- *more easily tired than peers*
- *more prone to examination stress*
- *often difficulty with a foreign language*
- *often better at practical subjects*
- *emotional and behavioural difficulties due to lack of motivation and lowered self-esteem*

What if I suspect my child is dyslexic?

If there are signs that your child is dyslexic, it is important to share your concerns with the class teacher and SENCo, who will follow procedures outlined by the Code of Practice. Your local dyslexia association can also provide you with further information. The possibility of an assessment through the LEA or privately may be discussed. An assessment will provide a profile of cognitive abilities and educational attainments, identify areas of strengths and weaknesses, and recommend avenues for support. Sometimes, access arrangements for examinations may be indicated. An assessment can be carried out by an Educational Psychologist or a Qualified Specialist Teacher holding a Practising Certificate. A Directory of Chartered Psychologists is available from the British Psychological Society (BPS) and a Directory of qualified Specialist Teachers from the Professional Association of Teachers of Students with Specific Learning Difficulties (PATOSS). Private assessments can also be arranged through organisations such as The Helen Arkell Dyslexia Centre.

How do I obtain information about dyslexia provision offered by prospective schools?

A useful resource is the Council for the Registration of Schools Teaching Dyslexic Pupils (CReSTeD). It offers a list of schools, organised by area, with varying levels of provision for students with dyslexia and other types of SPLD (i.e.

dyspraxia, dyscalculia, ADD, Asperger's). It includes independent and maintained schools with six levels of provision: Dyslexia Specialist Provision Schools, Specialist Provision Schools (for dyslexia and other associated difficulties), Dyslexia Units within schools, Specialist Classes (usually for English and Mathematics), Withdrawal System (whereby pupils are withdrawn for support) and Maintained Sector (whereby schools support dyslexic pupils across the curriculum). The registration list is updated regularly. A school's registration with CReSTeD is voluntary; therefore, the list is not exhaustive. An additional resource is the Schools for Special Needs (2011), which provides information as well as an index of schools according to need. It will be essential to obtain prospectuses from these and other prospective schools, view school websites, attend Open Days, and make direct contact with learning support departments to discuss your child's needs.

What questions should I ask when considering a secondary school?

Parents should prepare a list of questions when visiting and considering potential secondary schools. These questions will pertain to the ethos of the school, the type and level of support on offer, and curriculum choices. As for all learners, it is also important to include questions regarding pastoral care, teaching techniques, and areas that will build upon your child's current strengths and interests (for example, in music, drama, art, sport) or other areas of potential interest to your child. In Choosing a School for a Child with Special Needs, Birnbaum (2010) provides a comprehensive list of questions, also summarised on the CReSTeD website.

Relevant questions might include:

- *Is the curriculum differentiated for dyslexic students? If so, how?*
- *Are expectations high and how is classroom teaching made accessible to dyslexic learners?*

- *What type of extra support is offered and how is it delivered?*
- *Does provision go beyond literacy skills and include revision and study skills?*
- *Is any specialist equipment routinely used (e.g. word processor)?*
- *Does staff have specialist training in dyslexia?*
- *Is there flexibility in curriculum choices and examination boards (especially with regard to foreign languages)?*

How do I choose the 'right' school for my child?

In making decisions about the best school for your child, the criteria you set may differ from that of others. You may want a smaller school, smaller class sizes, a differentiated curriculum, hands-on learning techniques, additional support and/or use of technology (e.g. word processors), or a school in which specific curricular and extracurricular activities are prioritised - in essence, a place for YOUR child to be happy and thrive, where his unique talents are nurtured, with the right blend of expectation and support, and an environment where he will be engaged and motivated.

A diagnosis of dyslexia can often be the beginning of positive redirection. Your child has been struggling; now you have more information as to why. An assessment may reveal strengths in addition to weaknesses, and set in motion a set of strategies for support. It can improve motivation and self-esteem by helping your child understand why certain academic tasks are difficult for him, that many bright and capable people are dyslexic, and that strategies can be put in place to support his learning. Dyslexia is best viewed as a learning difference, a type of cerebrodiversity, which is likely to confer advantages as well as disadvantages for learning. An understanding of this learning difference is essential for choosing a supportive educational environment in which your child can thrive.

References:

Birnbaum, R. (2010). *Choosing a School for a Child with Special Needs.* London: Jessica Kingsley Publishers.

Cogan, J. & Flecker, M. (2004). *Dyslexia in Secondary School.* London: Whurr.

Pennington, B. (2009). *Diagnosing Learning Disorders, 2nd ed.* New York: Guilford Press.

Sherman, G.F. & Cowen, C.D. (2003, Spring). *Neuroanatomy of dyslexia through the lens of cerebrodiversity: The value of different thinkers in our midst.* Perspectives (International Dyslexia Association).

Resources:

The Council for the Registration of Schools Teaching Dyslexic Pupils (CreSTeD) *(www.crested.org.uk)*

Gabbitas Education (2011), *Schools for Special Needs, 17th ed.* London: Gabbitas.

The British Dyslexia Association *(www.bdadyslexia.org.uk)*

Office for Advice Assistance Support and Information on Special Needs *(www.oaasis.co.uk)*

The Helen Arkell Dyslexia Centre, Frensham, Farnham, Surrey GU10 3BL *(www.arkellcentre.org.uk)*

COMMON ENTRANCE

If your child moves to the prep system they will usually have to take a pre-test exam at 11 and a 'common entrance' exam at 13 but the prep system is very supportive with school choices.

The common entrance procedure is often unfamiliar to the state school family so we have included an explanation published on the Downsend school website.

The Common Entrance examinations are used for assessing pupils who transfer to many senior independent schools at 13. Most candidates take their Common Entrance papers in June of the year of entry to their senior school.

Examiners, appointed by the Independent Schools Examination Board (ISEB), set the Common Entrance papers, but the answers are marked by the senior school for which a candidate is entered. The Common Entrance papers consist of written papers in the following subjects: English, Maths, Science, French, History, Geography, Religious Studies and, if appropriate, Latin.

Common Entrance is essentially non-competitive, in that if a candidate reaches the required standard then a place will be given. Some schools however, are now awarding academic exhibitions to those pupils who produce the best overall Common Entrance score at the school.

As a general principle, better grades at Common Entrance will improve the possibility of candidates being put into higher 'sets' when they enter their senior school. Our expectation is therefore not simply to pass, but to do well in the Common Entrance exams.

ARTICLE: When and Where To Go

By Andrew Gough, Headmaster, Ripley Court School (mixed, independent preparatory school), Ripley, Surrey

Independent senior schools traditionally take boys at thirteen and girls at eleven, although this does vary from school to school. Advocates of 13+ suggest that the children should be just that little more mature and confident, before they are thrown into a mixing pot with chunky 18-year-olds floating about. This may be more important for boys, and less for girls, but without question 11-year-olds are very "young" when they leave primary schools. When it comes to entry tests there is actually a marked gender difference at 11+ too. This seems to iron itself out by 13. 11-year-old boys are often less socially mature than their female peers, and this does come through in the way, for example, that they write creative writing essays. At the risk of stereotyping, ask a girl what she did over the weekend and you are likely to get a long and detailed answer: "Well, we went to Guildford and we went up the High Street, and we saw Emily and then we decided to go for a coffee..." Ask a boy of a similar age the same question and you will get, "We went to Guildford." No more need be said – after all, you have been to Guildford too, and you know what it contains? I won't bore you with detail!

Advocates of single sex education would cite this as a good reason for separating the genders. I would use the same argument to point out that it is useful in life to get a handle on how the other half thinks. You live and deal with them everywhere else in life – so why insert your children into an artificial world just when they are learning social skills? After all, it is mostly in British and Empire schools, or convents, monasteries and prisons, that one has an artificial gender separation. It doesn't happen much elsewhere.

So what is the best age for a child to enter a senior school? Without question the correct time is the time when it starts. If all children go at 11+ then probably it is a good idea to start

with the gang. If they all go at 13+, then ditto. Unhelpfully, some schools have a split entry – so which is the better choice then? Probably to leave at the top of your primary school, which is likely to be at 11 from the state sector but may well be at 13 from an Independent Prep school. Remember that being at the top of a school is beneficial for all sorts of reasons – leadership, responsibility and the rest. One doesn't have many opportunities to be at the top of the pile in life, so don't rob your child of that one.

This book attempts to guide you in choosing a school for your child. Let me add to that by unpeeling some myths about selective entry into Senior Independent Schools in this country. Then, we'll look at a few strategies that are useful in approaching this.

Myth 1: *There is an absolute academic standard for entry.*

Firstly, all schools differ in their requirements and the skills they emphasize.

Secondly, within the same school there are variations year-on-year. Some Senior heads will argue vociferously that there is no variation, but I know how clever the children that I am sending them are, and I have always noted in every school that I have sent children to that there is a variation year-on-year. The reality of life is that few schools can afford to start a year with a shortage of pupils – this translates as a gap in the finances. A single empty seat will cost a senior school between £75k and £150k over five years. This is a lot of money. So:

Reality 1: *If a school has 100 entrants at whatever age they start, then they will select the top 100 entrants. This means that there may well be a considerable difference between the ability of the bottom entrants in any two successive years. The top entrants will usually be very bright. There are, therefore, elements of luck and the wider economy that affect your child's entry.*

Myth 2: *Children from state schools have an equal chance as those from prep schools.*

Reality 2: Children from Independent Prep schools have usually been prepared accurately for years for entry tests. There is no reason why state school children should not do well, but their schools will not prepare them as well, and there is a considerable body of expertise and knowledge in Prep schools which is hard to beat, so it is not a level playing field.

Importantly, the heads of prep schools spend considerable time with the heads of senior schools, so they are able to help you to target possible schools better. It is quite a slick and sophisticated system – this is part of what you are paying for.

Myth 3: A good school will make children cleverer.

Reality 3: A good school will enable children to perform better than a weak school, but otherwise you are born with what you've got. Excessive fish oil treatment and similar may raise your IQ a point or two – but these surveys are highly tendentious and there are many confounding variables (such as a child receiving proper nutrition for the first time in its life) which may explain away any such gains. You children are the product of your genes and there is nothing you can do about it.

That said, the fun in bringing up and teaching children is you don't know what they have got because they don't come labelled like a tin – so it is a huge kick to discover their various talents. In fact, that is a major reason why I do the job I do.

Myth 4: An independent school can sort out the problems that my child is having.

Reality 4: Myth 4 is wrong and right on several counts:

a. See myth 3. If your child is failing academically in any school it may well be that they are not very able.

b. If your child has special needs to the point where they are 'statemented', you should stay in the state system. Frankly, you get much better support.

c. If your child has a mild special need of the sort that attracts no funding in a state school then you are better off in an Independent school. Be aware, though, that you may well have to pay for the extra support – special needs in general are expensive.

d. If your child has behavioural problems and the independent school gets the vaguest hint of this, then they won't have them.

e. If your child is normal, quiet and no trouble, but not very assertive, you may find that they are lost in a big state school class. Your child may well be left to get on with it while the teacher concentrates on the "target" groups, such as gifted, special needs, behaviourally challenged 'characters' or similar. Most independent schools have classes that are too small to hide in and so getting lost at the back is unlikely to be an option.

Myth 5. *The policy on inclusion has worked well for the majority of children.*

Reality 5. *The policy of inclusion has been the single best thing any government could have thought of for swelling the demand for independent school places.*

You may be reading this because your child is not in a Prep school and so you cannot call on the advice of their headteacher.

Which senior schools should you target?

1. League tables do indicate good schools, but mostly only indicate the ability to select the intake, and the ability to deselect poor candidates later on, by hoofing them out before GCSEs or not allowing them into the 6th form. This hoofing is not public or peremptory – it takes the form of a quiet hand on the elbow, and it is very common amongst top league table performers.

2. Try to get an idea of how bright your child is really. You can get tests for this online or in bookshops, or the teachers might give you some advice. Remember myths 1 and 3.

3. The most popular and selective schools are usually popular because they are 'good' schools but mostly because they are cheaper than the others. Senior school fees can vary from £12k per year to £30k per year – a very considerable difference.

4. If you live in the greater London area, mainstream independent schools will not often take boys less than 60th centile in ability although there are some more specialist schools which will. Girls tend to be much easier to find schools for because there is an oversupply of girls schools, largely caused by more boys schools (than girls schools) having gone co-ed. I believe these effects are also noticeable in Birmingham and Manchester.

5. If you live more than 40 miles from Westminster, you will find a notable slacking off in the entry requirements. It is simple economics.

6. Most important, find someone who knows the local area. The most knowledgeable are prep school heads who prepare and feed to a variety of senior schools, then try to pick his or her brain – although they won't know what your child is like, they will know the local area. Tutors who specialise in getting state school children into independent schools will also have this knowledge.

Finally, as is stated elsewhere in this book, by all means prep your child for their entry, but don't overdo the coaching. If a child has to be excessively coached in order to gain entry, they will fall back as soon as the extra stops – possibly right out of the pattern. Ideally, you want to place your child in a school where they are not in the bottom quartile of the pack. Being at the bottom is a miserable place for any child.

6th Form

6th form may seem a long way away when you are researching schools if your eldest child is aged 9, but if you feel very strongly that you would like your child to stay in the same school throughout, it needs further thought.

- **A levels** are divided into 2 years with the AS level taken at the end of the first year. Children take between 3 and 5 A levels. Passes are graded between A and E. A* is awarded to those who score 90% or more. A levels translate into UCAS points.

- **The International Baccalaureate** is also a 2 year qualification but is recognised internationally for University application. This is a broader course than the A level. Students study 6 courses including a language, science and humanities from an international perspective. There is also a 'core' which includes 150 hours of creativity to include the arts, sport and service to the community.

- **The Cambridge Pre–U**. This is a new post-16 diploma developed by the Cambridge University. Some think that it is a better qualification than the A level which has received bad press in recent years. Pupils can choose a minimum of 3 subjects which can be broken down into smaller subjects. A Global Perspectives & Research course must be taken to gain the full diploma. This is to highlight independent learning.

Included here is an article about the IB. We have not included anything further about A levels as most of you will be familiar with them and may have taken them yourselves many years ago!

ARTICLE: Intellect Broadening

By Simon Powell, Director of School Development, Box Hill School

The International Baccalaureate Diploma was first taught in 1968 and has grown considerably as a form of sixth-form education – both nationally and internationally. In November 2006, former Prime Minister Tony Blair stated that he wished to see an IB school in every local authority, and an increasing number of schools, both independent and state, now offer it. Box Hill School is one of the schools in the South of England to have made the move.

As a qualification, the International Baccalaureate Diploma Programme overcomes one of the major criticisms of A Levels; it does not require students to specialise too early.

This appeals to university registrars and prospective employers as students taking the IB have a far broader range of skills. In a world where employers can be far more selective when it comes to appointing staff, the greater breadth of skills an employee can offer – competence in a foreign language for instance – can give students the edge. Box Hill School took the decision to switch to the International Baccalaureate Diploma from A Level with effect from September 2008 in order to give its students that edge.

One of the myths about IB is that it is only for the brightest, but this is a misrepresentation of the facts. It is true that there is a lot of work involved with the IB and students do need to be organised and manage their time well to keep on top of the work. The academic level in a student's three Higher Level subjects equates to that of three A Levels and their three Standard Level subjects are pitched somewhere between GCSE and AS level. However, as one student has said, "it is easier to manage your time with the IB as you learn from the start that you can't leave things until the last minute; work needs to be done as and when you can do it and you don't get into the mindset that you will be able to do it later." It is this work ethic that universities and employers will demand, and the structure of the IB course and the guidance given throughout will help students develop these valuable time-management skills.

For overseas students, who may consider that the IB requires more work, there are more compelling arguments for considering this as their qualification of choice. Without doubt it is seen as a much more 'International' qualification and as such is much more portable in terms of application to University in countries around the world. As a part of the course students have to study their native language and a second language (English when studying in the UK), and both of these elements count towards their overall IB grade. This is not the case with A Level, where Universities do not count native language in terms of UCAS points and the IELTS qualification at 6.5 or above is merely a pre-requisite for entry. It makes much more educational sense for students to continue to study some element of their native language and literature and gain credit for that study.

The IB however is not all work and no play: quite the contrary, as it expects students to complete CAS (Creativity, Action and Service) hours over the course. This means that involvement in sport, the performing and creative arts and community service, or service of any kind, is recognised and valued. This in itself says a great deal about the students and the diverse range of skills they can ultimately offer. The idea of a 'rounded education' where students do not focus solely on the academic is one that Box Hill School has always espoused, and the IB fits very well with this ethos.

Students also undertake other useful and complimentary elements of the programme, including Theory of Knowledge where they will discuss and investigate the basis of knowledge and learning, and develop the ability to reflect critically on the role that knowledge plays in a global society. The premise is that this encourages students to become independent thinkers and develop the ability to question and act responsibly in an increasingly complex world.

Instilling all of these skills at sixth-form level will prepare students for university and in theory reduce the chance of them dropping out or struggling with the demands of the course. As with A Levels the IB might not be for every student, but it is certainly an option which should be seriously considered and is becoming more popular both with UK and overseas students. Any school offering the IB would be happy to discuss the options with any prospective student.

Frequently Asked Questions

How do I know if my child is suitable to go to a selective school?

There are so many selective schools with a wide range of standards. You will need to do some research or contact my consultancy service if you are in the Esher Area. Some of the private schools will accept children with a wide range of abilities, but the state grammar schools are very competitive and only accept children with the kind of exceptionally high marks only achieved by children who are very bright or have been intensively tutored for the exams, and in reality it is usually both conditions that apply! Your child's current school should be able to let you know the level that they are working at even if they are not happy to recommend schools. For example, if your child is achieving a level 4 in Maths and you find out that the school you like requires level 5 for the 11+, at least you know what you are aiming for. You will need to obtain the relevant information.

Do I need to find a tutor? Can I do it myself?

You can teach your child yourself but it depends on your relationship with your child. You will need to be both structured and encouraging and not stress each other! Please see our practice organiser in the section entitled 'Ready, Steady, Go!'. Some children will not cope with high-pressurised competitive tutoring. Choose a tutor by recommendation and not just by results. Do they know the local schools? Are they CRB checked?

Should I practise 'standard' or 'multiple choice' papers?

Standard papers do not give options of answers which means that while the child is learning to do verbal and non-verbal reasoning they cannot guess the answers.

It is better to practise 'standard' first so that the pupil can work out the answer properly and not jump to conclusions from the answer sheet. Once they are confident they can then use 'multiple choice', and this will actually help with the speed by quickly eliminating wrong answers.

Find out whether the school uses standard or multiple choice.

Have I left it too late to start practising? Can you do 11+ in 11 weeks? How about 11 days?

2 ½ terms or 11 months tends to be the most popular amount. It can be done in a term, but for all but the most gifted children they will have to be more committed, doing a paper a day instead of a bit once a

week. If your exam is next week then, as a minimum, buy some practice papers and check that your child understands how to answer the questions (see recommendations).

If your child needs more than a year's tutoring you are probably looking at the wrong school!

What marks should my child achieve?

This is a bit of a 'how long is a piece of string' question. It depends on the school. I (Anita) tend to make sure that all my pupils can achieve 85%, but some of the more competitive schools need high 90%s; conversely some schools are happy with 60%. It tends to relate to how academic the school is perceived to be.

My child is working too slowly. What can I do?

You can practise groups of questions with a timer. Generally it is a good idea to practise 30 seconds per question. For example, 20 questions in 10 minutes. Most of the practice papers have 85 questions in 50 minutes, some may have 100 and some a shorter number where the reasoning is included with the Maths and English. The schools will not generally tell you the actual format.

My child is dyslexic. Will they be capable of doing the exam?

Obviously there is a range of dyslexia. A child who is very dyslexic may have to go to a specialist school, but there are very bright dyslexic pupils who can be high achievers. Generally dyslexic pupils need more repetition, and if their vocabulary is limited they may find some of the verbal questions difficult. Many dyslexic pupils will qualify for an extra 25% of time for the exam with an educational psychologist's report.

However, look into the support they will receive once at the school!

Myths and Misnomers about Verbal and Non-Verbal Reasoning

Myth 1: Reasoning tests are all about IQ, and hence you cannot improve your score with practice.

The truth: You CAN learn to do reasoning and improve your result through practice because it is about confidence, experience and speed - not just raw intelligence. I sometimes hear, "My child is bright; he doesn't need any practice." There are many bright children all having tutoring and further refining their ability so he/she will be at a disadvantage not to have done any practice at all. Many selective schools are very competitive.

Myth 2: Verbal reasoning is all about words.
The truth: Verbal reasoning does indeed involve words, but it also includes Maths problems as it is all about written puzzles (letters and numbers) rather than pictorial puzzles (non-verbal).

Myth 3: Non-verbal reasoning is all about Maths.
The truth: Non-verbal reasoning involves finding relationships between pictorial shapes or diagrams. Number-based puzzles are included in verbal reasoning (see Myth 2).

Myth 4: It is very expensive to get my child adequately prepared for entrance exams.
The truth: Whilst paying for tutoring expertise clearly does cost, practising reasoning with your child does not have to be very expensive. You can help them yourself with structured practice, encouragement and rewards (just as a school does) and buy packs of papers with sample tests for just a few pounds. There are also some free online tests.

Myth 5: My child's school will cover all of the work that they need.
The truth: Actually, many state schools do not do any verbal and non-verbal at all, especially in an area which is not a grammar school area. Prep schools, however, do prepare children for the 11+ pre-test although my observation is that if you want to transfer out of a prep school and into a secondary school in year 7 then you may need to do more practice and preparation than the prep schools provide.

Myth 6: My child is capable of choosing their own school.

The truth: This one is ridiculous yet sadly all too commonly voiced. At the age of 10 children do NOT have the ability to understand the bigger picture of their choices at all. They will choose it on the basis of something such as friendship groups or flashy facilities almost every time. Do not underestimate the desire to remain with their friends as it is usually stronger than anything else and hence clouds their judgement. They are also easily swayed by peer pressure and rumours about the school. One misunderstood comment from a teacher or older pupil will put them off at an Open Day so do not allow them to think they have too much choice in the matter. Explain your choices to them and listen to their concerns but do not let them dictate.

Success is the good fortune that comes from aspiration, desperation,
perspiration and inspiration
– Evan Esar.

B. Reasonable Reasoning

Many schools in both state and independent sectors use 'reasoning' tests as part of their assessment process. As we have already discussed, even a bright child needs at least some practice at these to be sure of doing well.

In this section we have included both verbal and non-verbal reasoning GL style examples. Even if they are not relevant to you for your child's entrance exam why not cut them out and take them to restaurants for fun. We know that our children always liked something to do whilst waiting for food and it is a bit more sociable than playing on your mobile phone! Children love that their parents don't immediately know the answers either and have to work them out as well. We often find that this time builds 'dads and daughters' relationships as mums sometimes believe that dads are better at the non-verbal in particular – sorry to stereotype!

For the verbal reasoning (including verbal Maths) we have included an example, tips and hints, and a couple of practice questions of each type. This is a brief introduction to the techniques which will need to be followed up with practice papers. It is in enough depth for you as a parent to understand what the children have to do if you are tutoring your child yourself.

In order to achieve high scores a good vocabulary is essential. Please encourage your child to read a lot and note down words that they do not know AND learn them. We have included some words after the non-verbal as a starting point for their vocabulary list. They need to become used to using a dictionary and thesaurus to develop their learning.

The non-verbal reasoning includes examples of the seven most popular types of questions with examples provided by Eleven Plus Exams (**www.elevenplusexams.co.uk**).

Non-verbal reasoning looks complicated but is not as confusing as you may at first think. There are only so many things that you can do to a shape! Children can achieve high scores in non-verbal by carefully following the rules.

- Sometimes the 'colour' of the shape is changed. They are only ever printed in black and white so 'colour' means they are either black, white or shaded in a particular way such as striped or spotted etc.;

- They may be rotated in an interesting way. They could be rotated clockwise, anti-clockwise or reflected/flipped (use a mirror if you get stuck with this while you are learning the technique);

- Questions sometimes require an understanding of symmetry, such as the number of lines of symmetry, or you may have to spot the odd one out where a series of shapes are all symmetrical except one;

- It is important to understand angles. To understand a right angle compare with the corner of a desk. An obtuse angle is bigger than a right angle (imagine the hands showing 4 o' clock on a clock face), and an acute angle is smaller than a right angle (imagine 2 o'clock on a clock face);

- Codes are also widely used. Always start by looking at what is similar. If there are two 'W's look at what is similar between the two shapes (colour, position, etc.);

- Position is very important. Shapes can move around from one box to the next. The outer shape can become the inner shape and so on. Sometimes in serial relationships the pattern can be tracked every other box;

- Count! Sometimes it is just a simple counting exercise. Always count lines, dots, shapes, etc. and compare from box to box. One less, one more, even numbers, odd numbers and all manner of permutations;

- Don't be put off! The harder questions always seem to have something to make it seem more complicated: arrows and wiggly lines are introduced for no reason. It is, however, very easy to over-complicate these questions.

Other types of non-verbal reasoning types of questions include:

- Cubes;

    1. The cube is rotated and seen from a different angle. The pupil has to find the correct cube;
    2. Which cube can be made from the given net (a net is a 2 dimensional pattern that when folded up will make a three dimensional shape).

- Find an identical part within a muddled shape;
- Find which three out of four shapes can make the new shape.

It is a good idea to look at different types of papers and even puzzle books so your child is not thrown by new concepts. Note that the schools ask companies to prepare their exam papers so they are not always in the same format that you can buy at the shops. Recently one pupil said to Anita, "There was a section that was completely different from how you taught us." His friend replied, "No it wasn't; it was just set out in a different way."

Remember, schools DO NOT want applicants to be over-tutored, and some do not really want tutoring to take place at all. Of course they have to stay one step ahead of parents' strategies for gaining competitive advantage. They want to see children's intelligence and adaptability. Of course the exam papers are not always going to look the same as those found on the High Street. Your child needs to be prepared for this and not locked into one style of working over a year or more - they will be lost when required to actually 'think' in a way that may be 'outside the box'.

Verbal Reasoning Language Techniques

Crack the Code!

TECHNIQUE 1

Fill in the missing word needed to complete the third pair of words. This pair follows the same pattern as the first two pairs of words.

Hint: Sometimes you will need to number the letters to help solve a complicated question.

1 2 3 4 / 2 1 3 4	*1 2 3 4 / 2 1 3 4*	*1 2 3 4 / 2 1 3 4*
RAID ARID	*MAID AMID*	*ABLE BALE*

trail / rail	**brake / rake**	**erode /**
shoe / hose	**teas / eats**	**seat /**

TECHNIQUE 2

In the following there are two sets of words. The word in brackets on the left hand side has been formed using some of the letters of the words on the either side of its brackets. You must write the missing word in the brackets on the right hand side which can be formed from its pair of words in the same way. Therefore you need to find the pattern of letters in the first set of words and apply the same pattern to the second set.

Hint: Number the left-hand word and put letters above the right-hand word.

<pre>
              b   b
    1 2 3 4   1 2 c d   a b c d   1 2 3 4 1 2 c d   a b c d
E.g. M I S T (M I L K) S I L K   D R A W (D L I P) F L I P
                                          (D R I P)
</pre>

Note that in the example above there are two possible solutions as the letter 'I' could be taken from either the first or the last word, i.e. letter position *2* from the first word or letter position *b* from the third word. However, only one of these actually makes a valid new word for the second group of words.

Now try these:

FIND (FIGS) HUGS	MARK ( ) LIST
SOLD (SILT) DIRT	PILL ( ) MARE

TECHNIQUE 3

Using the alphabet to help you continue the letter series in each of the examples below and fill in the empty brackets.

A B C D E F G H I J K L M N O P Q R S T U V W X Y Z   A B C...

+3   +3   +3   +3
R   U   X   A   D   (G)

Remember to go back to the beginning of the alphabet once you get to Z.

-2   -2   -2   -2
P   N   L   J   H   (F)

You can count backwards as well.

In the following example there are 2 letters in each group. If you are given 2 letters, go from the first of the first pair to the first of each pair in each group. Similarly go from the second of the pair to the second of the pair in each group.

+1   +2   +3
Q K   R C   T W   W S   (A Q)
-8   -6   -4

N.B. The numbers for the first letters are at the top and the numbers for the second letter are at the bottom.

The following example shows a different pattern. Don't dive in too quickly in case there isn't an obvious pattern. In this instance you can jump 2 groups.

A F   Z X   **B** H   Y U   (**C** J)

Draw arrows over the top to help see the pattern

The one below shows a different pattern again. To solve this one you have to notice the two interwoven patterns. See the letters in bold and compare with the remaining letters and you will see both patterns.

O   **A**   **B**   P   **C**   **D**   Q   **E**   **(F)**   (R)

Now try these:

N   **P**   **S**   **W**   **B**   (   )

J A   **H D**   **F G**   **D J**   **B M**   (   )

Puzzling Puzzles!

TECHNIQUE 1

Each of the following has a word with its letters jumbled up. Using the 'clue' rearrange the letters and write the correct words in brackets.

> *Hint: Write the word in a circle. Look at the 'clue' and go through all the possible words.*

Example: BIGNOWL
Clue: I go out and do this activity with my friends on Saturday nights.

(What are the possibilities? Go through them in your head.)

```
    B     I
 L           G
   W       N
       O
```

T I B O B H	**A small person with hairy feet known for collecting magical rings**
T O P R E T	**Someone who makes clay objects – also a famous wizard**

If you have not met these characters yet, you need to be acquainted. The first is the star of one of the greatest selling books in the world, recently made into a film trilogy.

The second series of books are also bestselling books. If you find reading challenging, watch the films first. They are good books to talk about in your interview as your interviewer will know them.

TECHNIQUE 2

In the following questions write in the brackets the ONE letter which will finish the first word and begin the second word of each pair. The same letter is used for both pairs of words.

Hint: Concentrate on one word at a time. Check to see if it fits with another one. If you are really stuck, you will have to go through the alphabet a letter at a time.

E.g. TREND (Y) OU   BRAIN (Y) ES

H I ( ) A R T Y	**C A ( ) R I M R O S E ***
C O O ( ) A P T O P	**W O O ( ) E V E R E T ****

* Learn the names of common flowers and trees. How many yellow flowers can you name?

** Make sure you also learn the names of baby animals. What is a baby swan called? How about female versions of animals? What is a female sheep called? And a female or male deer?

TECHNIQUE 3

One letter from the left-hand word must be taken and placed into the word on the right-hand side so that TWO new proper words are formed which are correctly spelt. All the other letters of the words must remain in the same position.

Example: KNIT and PIE become NIT and PIKE

This type of nit is found in your hair – arrgh!

Hint: Cover each letter of the first word with a pencil. Once you have made a new word put the letter in the next word in each possible place.

K N I T

K PIE   P **K** I E   P I **K** E   P I E **K**

N.B. Remember to make a note of words that you don't know. A pike is a fresh water fish with a long snout. Types of fish often appear in 11+ questions.

SNOUT and TROT become _____ and _____

SWEAT and SAT become _____ and _____

This first one is a real word but don't go looking for street slang, 'swear' words or proper nouns. You won't find them, and if they are there it was obviously a mistake! ☺

A 'proper noun' is the specific name of something or someone (like London, Anita or Peugeot) and always starts with a capital letter.

TECHNIQUE 4

In each of the following questions you must change the top word into the bottom word by changing one letter at a time until you get the bottom word. Each time you change a letter you need to make another valid word. The example below requires just one additional step but be aware that some questions require further additional steps to get to the solution.

> *Hint: Write in the two letters that are the same. Try changing one of the others. If it does not make a sensible word try changing the other one.*

Example:

TASK	TASK	TASK		TASK
---------	A K	WASK (not a real word)		TALK
WALK	WALK	WALK		WALK

TECHNIQUE 5

One of the words in each of the following sentences has three consecutive letters missing. Without changing the order of these three letters they spell another word. Write this word in the brackets.

If you do a lot of texting on your mobile phone you will love this one!

> *Hint: Once you have guessed the word write it out over the top. Cross out the letters that are given. The remaining 3 letters should spell a word. This is your answer.*

Reasoning

E.g. I love verbal reaing = son

I buy DVDs with my ALANCE (   )
Clue: similar to pocket money

He SHED at his sister (   )

Sort the Sentence!

TECHNIQUE 1

In each of the following there is the SAME connection between the word outside each set of brackets and one word inside each set of brackets. You must find this same connection and then underline the TWO words, one from each set of brackets.

Hint: Put the word in a sentence using the same 'connection' words.

Example: elephant is to (trunk, grey, Africa)
as cow is to (milk, udder, farm)

Elephants **have** trunks and cows **have** udders **as parts of their body**.

Work this out by considering the various options:

Elephants are grey.   Cows are (colour?)   So 'grey' does not work.

Some pupils may choose 'Africa' and 'farm' with 'live' as the connection word but this is wrong because 'Africa' is a specific geographical place where one might find elephants whereas 'farm' is a generic location and hence 'trunk' and 'udder' is a better fit.

- **Computer game is to (play, disc, score) as MP3 player is to (headphones, music, listen)**
- **Hair is to (head, plait, dye) as nail is to (varnish, cut, hammer)**

Sometimes these words are based on spellings (homophones and heterographs) such as MIST and MISSED; sometimes letters are added such as BAND and BRAND or even spelt backwards as in MEET and TEEM.

TECHNIQUE 2

Underline the 2 words which should change places with each other in order to make sense of the following sentences.

Hint:　　*Look away - what is this trying to say?*

Example:　The <u>girl</u> licked the <u>dog</u>

No monkey in the feeding enclosure
Fifty three and thirty one make twenty four

Beware of something like: <u>It</u> <u>is</u> football today? The punctuation gives you the clue you need to get this right.

A Word or Two!

TECHNIQUE 1

Find the FOUR letter word which is hidden in each of the following sentences. Each four letter word can be found by studying the letters at the end of one word and the beginning of the next word. Write this word in the brackets.

This could be 1 letter from one word + 3 letters from the next or   2 + 2 or 3 + 1

Hint: Move your finger across the words to spot the beginning of the word.

1+3

Example: She fell head over heels in love = dove

Beware of the second practice question below which I have put in to stretch you a bit! There are two possible answers and each one is spread over three words (which sometimes happens).

- **Fast cars and high-speed trains are cool**
- **Mum is terribly cross as I got lost in the fog (2 possible answers)**

TECHNIQUE 2

A word from the left-hand group will join together with a word from the right-hand group to form a completely new and proper word. The word from the left-hand group always begins this new word. Underline the two words, one from each group.

Hint: Always work in order; first to first, first to second etc.

Example: rabbit/quid/drainage   note/hole/ditch
= quidditch™ (the game played by Harry Potter™)

To all you 'muggles™' out there, don't worry – words from fictional books won't come up – I'm just trying to keep you interested! ☺

Beware: The words don't always sound as they are written. You may have to write out the whole word if you are stuck, e.g. so - lid, fat - her, is - land.

Also: It must be one word, not a word with a hyphen.

Try these:

• **sun/super/first**	**rays/class/star**
• **quite/extra/less**	**normal/known/ordinary**

Harry Potter™ and Muggle™ and Quidditch™ are trademarks of Time Warner Entertainment Company L.P. and other entities.

TECHNIQUE 3

Underline one word in each pair of brackets to make the most sensible sentence.

Hint: Look for clue words, for example, 'repaired' in the first example.

Example: The (<u>plumber</u>, doctor, magician) *repaired* the (<u>toilet</u>, rabbit, leg) in the (hat, supermarket, <u>church</u>).

- **The (boy, doctor, cat) texted his (patient, girlfriend, chicken) to ask for a (date, banana, worm)**

- **(If, When, How) Jake went to the (park, frog, movie) he took his (dog, carrot, heart)**

Thanks to Sebastian from a recent year 5 group for the second question. Can you make up one as well?

Vocabulary Vortex!

TECHNIQUE 1

Underline TWO words in the brackets which have the SAME or nearly the same meaning as the word in capitals outside the brackets.

> *Hint: Put the words in the same sentence to check that the meaning is similar.*

> *Example:* PARK (playground gardener field pavilion)

A park is an open space where you can play, and so is a playground and a field.

One word which doesn't fit is 'gardener'. 'Garden', however, would have fitted. 'Pavilion' also doesn't fit as this is a building which is found by a cricket pitch or recreational ground.

> *Hint: Even if you do not know the meaning of the words notice if they are nouns, verbs etc.*

Note: Sometimes the format of this type of question varies. You might be asked to find similar words, opposite words, one word, two words, or in the case of the questions in the box below, you have to find the two words which do not belong.

Underline the two words which do not fit with the meaning.

- **MEANDER (saunter, lolloping, traipse, roam, lunge)**
- **STUTTER (murmur, mutter, stammer, articulation, shriek)**

- You can 'spice' up your writing by learning words to describe how different people walk or talk.

- People often fall down on this section because they do not know the vocabulary. Make a note of any words you don't know and, most importantly, read a variety of books.

TECHNIQUE 2

There is a connection between the three items in capital letters before the brackets and TWO of the words inside the brackets. Underline the TWO words.

Hint: Think of a group name for the words outside the brackets then find the missing one from the group.

Example:

HB PENCIL   PERMANENT MARKER   CHARCOAL...
Note: these are all writing/ drawing implements
(<u>felt tips</u>, clip art, <u>highlighter pen</u>, protractor, draw).

Beware: 'draw' is a verb.

Now try these:

- **GRUMPY   SULKY   GROUCHY**   (teenager, cantankerous, petulant, spotty, mood)
- **TRAINER FLIP-FLOPS   PUMPS** (hightops, heel, insole, welly, horseshoe)

Sometimes you need to find the closest meaning or opposite meaning between one word in each set of brackets.

In this case choose the two words, one from each set, that are the closest in meaning.

(miserable <u>miserly</u> irritated)   (uncomfortable <u>mean</u> masterful)
= miserly and mean   *'miserly' means selfish with money = stingy*

Sometimes you are given the words in brackets and then you have to find a new 'common' word that is not given – like this...

(syllables write)   (trance charm)   = spell

TECHNIQUE 3

Each of the following sets of brackets has ONE word which does NOT belong to the rest. Underline the 'odd one out'.

Example: (phone email videoconference play)

Play is the odd one out as the others are ways of communicating

Beware: Often the words are very closely linked. Think carefully! ☺

- (internet webpage computer cat mouse)
- (football badminton rugby netball basketball)

TECHNIQUE 4

Underline the word that would come in the middle if the following were put in order of size, sequence or position.

E.g. (child baby pensioner <u>adolescent</u> adult)

- (Kindle™ Apple-Mac™ Xbox™ iPad 2™ iPod-shuffle™) *[physical size]*
- (1p 50p £2.00 20p 5p)

No you will not get these as they are registered products, but it makes learning the techniques a bit more fun!

Look up these words below as they can crop up in the tests as part of this type of question. So, to make sure you are prepared, for each word below put it in a list (size, number) with four related words that you can find (use a dictionary and thesaurus to help you if necessary).

- Hamlet
- Tug
- Decimetre
- Dodecahedron
- Quartet
- Colonel
- Oboe
- Syllable
- Doe

A problem shared is a problem halved!

TECHNIQUE 1

This technique is all about the alphabet.

*Hint: Know that M is the **Middle** letter (M for **Middle**) 13th letter and T is the **Twentieth** letter (T for 20)*

These questions are often in several parts and you might wonder where to start. Sometimes it helps to draw a diagram.

What is the 3rd letter of the month which comes five months after the month which begins with the letter which is 3 letters after L in the alphabet?

Hint: Start from the end. What is 3 letters after L in the alphabet?

Look up and learn the 'Thirty days has September, April, June and November' rhyme if you don't already know it. Questions about the months of the year are popular!

Also learn these words:

- **Occurs** – means 'appears' or 'happens'. For example, "Which letter occurs three times?";
- **Frequently** – means that it happens regularly or often. For example, "The buses frequently break down";
- **Adjacent** – means next to something else. For example, "Your classroom is adjacent to mine";
- **Sequence** – means list in a specific, correct order. For example, "Put the numbers in sequence, starting with the lowest";
- **Series** – similar to *sequence*, means multiple items in a pattern or order. For example, "I watched all ten episodes in the series";

- **Consecutive** – means it happens one after the other. For example, "We have exams on consecutive days this week";
- **Combine** – means to join (two or more) things together. For example, "Combine two words to make another larger word";
- **Product** – used in maths to mean the result of multiplying numbers together;
- **Sum** – used in maths to mean the result of adding numbers together.

What are the five consecutive letters of the alphabet that occur in the word 'Cambridge'?

TECHNIQUE 2

You are given some information about five or six different items which often have alphabetical names. You are then asked questions.

Hint: The alphabetical names are your 'clue' to draw a quick chart which makes answering the questions very easy.

There are five friends called Alice, Bethany, Caitlin, Daisy and Emily. Alice, Caitlin and Daisy prefer going to the cinema while the others prefer ice-skating. Bethany, Caitlin and Emily are the only ones who like swimming. Bethany and Emily prefer to go out on Saturdays whereas the others prefer Sundays. Only Alice and Emily are allowed to travel alone. You need to help the girls plan how they use their weekends.

To solve this complicated puzzle I have drawn a little grid below. The details for each girl are put in one column and so now it is easy to answer the questions.

A	B	C	D	E
C	I	C	C	I
	S	S		S
Sun	Sat	Sun	Sun	Sat
Tr				Tr

1. How many children like swimming and can go out on Saturday?
2. Which child prefers Sunday and can travel to the cinema alone?
3. How many children prefer ice-skating and can go out on Saturday?
4. Which child prefers ice-skating and likes swimming but cannot travel alone?
5. Which child does not like swimming, does not like going out on Saturdays and cannot travel alone?
6. If the girls go ice-skating on Saturday who will go and who will need to ask for a lift with someone else?
7. Which girls could go to the cinema on Sunday? Out of those girls who will have to ask for a lift?

And now one for the boys...

Andrew, Ben, Chris, Dave and Ed all go to the same school. Andrew and Chris go on the bus on Mondays, Thursdays and Fridays. On Tuesdays and Wednesdays when they don't have to carry their sports gear they go through the woods to school on their mountain bikes. Dave (who thinks he's cool!) goes to school on his skateboard on Fridays. Ben and Ed go to school by scooter except for Mondays and Thursdays when they share lifts with their parents. Dave joins Ben and Ed on their scooters some days (only if it is not raining, otherwise his hair gel washes away!) but on Mondays and Thursdays he always takes the bus.

	A	**B**	**C**	**D**	**E**
Mon	Bus	Li	Bus	Bus	Li
Tue	Bi	Sc	Bi	Sc/Bus	Sc
Wed	Bi	Sc	Bi	Sc/Bus	Sc
Thu	Bus	Li	Bus	Bus	Li
Fri	Bus	Sc	Bus	SB	Sc

1. Which boy travels on his own one day a week?
2. Which days do most children travel on the bus?
3. How many children travel by scooter on Tuesdays?
4. How many times do children have lifts with parents?
5. Which children travel to school in the 'healthiest' way?
6. Do any children take the bus on Wednesdays?
7. Which day do the children have sport?

Break the Code

These are code questions. Have a go at writing a secret message to your friend, but don't forget to tell them how to crack the code. There are five types of questions most used.

CODE TYPE 1.

This usually involves counting forwards or backwards a number of letters to find the code.

Beware: If you have to find the code for a word you may have to count in one direction, but you may have to do the opposite for the answer if you have to work out the original word from the code word!

A B C D E F G H I J K L M N O P Q R S T U V W X Y Z

This alphabet will help you to find the example to the following code questions.

Example: The code word for Moon is OQQP. What is the real word for the code FCYP?

MOON   Code = OQQP   This is +2 for each letter.

(M + 2 places along the alphabet = O, etc.)

Code word: FCYP   As this is the code word you need to work out the original word so you must count backwards -2 for each letter.

Have you heard of the books New Moon and Breaking Dawn? They are part of the 'Twilight' series and girls love them!
Crack this code to find what these books are all about....

Hint: What has happened to each letter? J - 8 = B, R - 7 = L etc.

If JYKFOLPH = BREAKING then DHSUMUGT =

CODE TYPE 2.

This type of code question involves reversing the alphabet.

1 2   3   4...   ...23 24 25 26

A B   C D E F G H I J K   L M N O P Q R S T U V W X Y Z

26 25 24 23...   ...4   3   2   1

In these books there are also more than one of these creatures....

Example:

If GDRORTSG stands for TWILIGHT then VXORKHV stands for ECLIPSE

If   YRGV means BITE   then   DLOU means

CODE TYPE 3.

A series of books that boys often enjoy reading are about a hero called...?

For these questions you need to number each letter. The code is given as a number.

1 2 3 4...   ...23 24 25 26

A B C D E F G H I J K L M N O P Q R S T U V W X Y Z

Hint: 1 = A   2 = B etc

If HERO = 8,5,18,15   then:

- **16,5,18,3,25 =**

- **10,1,3,11,19,15,14 =**

CODE TYPE 4.

These can be tricky so here is an easy one to start with:

The following number codes 7648   4678   4567   4867 stand for MOAN MEAN NAME and MANE but not in the same order.

Start off by working out which code is for which word. They all start with 4 except for one which starts with 7. Therefore 7 must be the letter 'N' so 7648 must be NAME. That gives you 4 letters straight away. Can you do the rest?

What is the code for MOON?

What word is this the code for 7857?

CODE TYPE 5.

These codes do not rely on the order of the alphabet. Instead they give you words where letters are substituted for other letters at random. Using only that information you need to work out the answers.

Have you read the Stormbreaker series? Many boys enjoy these as well. Using the main character's name can you find the codes?

If WXYZ is the code for Alex and QRSYQ is the code for Rider find the codes for:

RELAX and READ

Hint: Write the code above the letters of the real word.

W	X	Y	Z	Q	R	S	Y	Q
A	L	E	X	R	I	D	E	R

And Now for Maths

In verbal reasoning papers there will be a variety of Maths problems, based on six different types of question.

Technique 1 - 'X' Marks The Spot – Fun With Algebra

Algebra is not taught in all schools at the age of 10 and 11 to the level required for most 11+ exams. Algebra is where a letter represents a number, such as x = 3

The principals to learn are:

- If there are two letters next to each other that means multiply.

For example: *ab* means *a* x *b* (*a* times *b*)

- *b*² means '*b*' multipled by itself (*b* squared) so if *b* is 3 then *b*² means 3 x 3

- *b*³ means *b* cubed or *b* x *b* x *b* so, *b* x *b* = 3 x 3 = 9 then you multiply the 9 by another 3 so the answer is 27.

- One above the other with a line between means divide:

$\frac{c}{b}$ means *c* divided by *b* (like a fraction) so if *c* is 12 and *b* is still 3 the sum would be 12 divided by 3 so the answer is 4.

- It is important that brackets are understood as well. Always work out the brackets first.

If you have *de* ÷ (*b* + *f*) work out *b* + *f* first, then *d* x *e*, then divide the first answer by the second answer.

Now try the first example below:

Beware: Make sure you notice whether the answer must be given as a letter or a number.

If $A = 6$, $B = 5$, $C = 4$, $D = 3$, $E = 2$, $F = 1$ what is the value of the following?

$de \div (b + f)$ **Give the answer as a letter**

$\dfrac{(ad - e)}{e}$ **Give the answer as a number**

Technique 2 – Number Series

In each of the following number series there is a different connection between the numbers. Find each connection and continue the series placing your answer in brackets (sometimes you need to fill in blanks within the number series).

Hint: Count the difference between each number.

Variation 1: Often the number pattern increases or decreases.

$$-10 \quad -9 \quad -8 \quad -7$$

Example: 51 41 32 24 ( )

Variation 2: Consider times tables

$$\times 2 \quad \times 3 \quad \times 4 \quad \times 5$$

Example: 2 4 12 48 ( )

Variation 3: Learn to recognise square numbers

Example: 16 25 36 49 64 ( )

Variation 4: Sometimes the first 2 numbers are added together to make the third etc and so on.

$$+ \quad = \quad + \quad = \quad + \quad =$$

Example: 0 1 1 2 3 5 8 ( )
so the next number would be 5 plus 8

Variation 5: Sometimes you may need to 'jump a number' to make the numbers make sense:

Example: **92** 14 **82** 18 **72** 22 ( ) ( )

You can see that 92 goes down 10 to 82 and that from 18 to 22 is +4 so there are 2 different patterns going on weaved together. When the pattern looks very complicated there is often an easier solution. What are the next two numbers in the series?

Now try these (the second one is harder but questions like this do come up!):

- 2   4   8   14   (   )
- 3   9   36   180   (   )

Technique 3 – Numerical Relationships

The mathematical relationship represented by the first set of numbers has to be applied to the second set to work out what goes in the brackets. Sometimes there are 3 sets of brackets where the first two are completed. If this is the case, use the middle set of brackets to check your 'rule'.

Example:　4　(10)　16　:　5　(**11**)　17　　*add 6 in each case*

Hint: Each set of numbers is essentially a three number series. Sometimes the series is just simple addition or subtraction working from left to right, but often it is more complex and involves using the numbers in a different order and perhaps with multiplication or division:

Example:　　6 (15) 9　　2 (**7**) 5
　　　　adding the first and last numbers equal the middle number

Try these:

- 8　(4)　4　:　12 (7)　5　:　9　(　　)　3
- 5 (565) 6　:　7 (787) 8　:　4　(　　)　5　*Look at the positions*

Technique 4 – Tabulated Data

You will be given a timetable or chart where you are asked questions about the data it contains. For example, look at the table below:

	Train A	Train B	Train C	Train D
Guildford	16:00	16:08	16:17	16:34
Surbiton	16:37	16:41	16:54	17:07
Wimbledon	16:49	16:50	17:04	17:20
Waterloo	17:07	17:10	17:22	17:37

1. I live in Wimbledon and catch the train to Guildford to go ice-skating and afterwards my Dad has arranged to pick me up from Wimbledon station at 5.00pm. What is the latest train that I can catch from Guildford?

2. Which train travels the quickest from Guildford to Waterloo?

3. Which 2 adjacent stations would you think are the furthest apart?

4. I leave school in Surbiton at 16:39 to go to Waterloo to meet a friend. If it takes me 7 minutes to walk to the station and then I take the next available train what time will I arrive at Waterloo?

Technique 5 – Maths Problem Solving

Verbal reasoning tests usually include miscellaneous mathematical problems.

Hint: If a problem is in several parts, deal with each part separately.
*To correct a watch that is slow you must add minutes **but** take the number away if you have to show the time on the watch! To correct a watch that is fast you must take away minutes **but** add the number to show the time on the watch! Draw diagrams if necessary. In age questions always work from **NOW**.*

Example:

I need to catch a train home but I am confused because my watch is 6 minutes slow. To make things worse, the train should have arrived at 2.18pm but I have been told by the station manager that it is running 11 minutes late. What time will my watch show when the train arrives?

Hint: If the train is late it is behind schedule. To calculate its arrival you must add on minutes. 2.18 + 11 = 2.29.

If my watch is slow what time does it say when the train arrives? You need to take 6 minutes off the time. 2.29 – 6 = 2.23   This is the answer.

- **Josh is three school years above James who is four years below Joseph.**

  What year is James in if Joseph will be in year 11 in two years time?
  Who is younger, Josh or James and by how many years?

- My mum is meant to be picking me up from school at 11.20 to go to a dentist's appointment but she phoned the school to say she is running ten minutes late. The clock in the classroom is 8 minutes fast and it currently says it is 10.51.

  How many minutes have I actually got before my mum gets to school?

Technique 6 – True Statements

In these questions you are asked to identify the only statement that must be true based on the information given.

Hint: Beware of words such as usually, frequently, might or could. You can't be certain that something happened.

Example:

Diversity, a dance troupe, won the third series of Britain's Got Talent. They just beat Susan Boyle in the live final. There are 12 members of the group with Ashley Banjo being the choreographer.

Based on the information you have been given above, which of the following are true?

1. Ashley studied sciences at university - *this may be true but it doesn't say*
2. Susan Boyle came 2nd in the live final - *true, as Diversity just beat her*
3. Diversity spend all their spare time dancing - *not necessarily!*
4. Ashley usually choreographs the dances - *beware of 'usually'*

2012 is the year of the Queen's Diamond Jubilee, the Olympics in Great Britain and Kate Middleton, the Duchess of Cambridge had her 30th Birthday. Underline one of the following answers that must be true:

1. 2012 is a momentous year for all.

2. The Queen is the longest reigning Monarch.

3. The Queen came to the throne in 1952.

4. The Duchess of Cambridge enjoyed her Birthday celebrations.

Non-Verbal Reasoning Logic Techniques

Each question type is presented for you on a separate page, with answers and explanation on the following page. This will enable you to cut out these pages and give them to your child to try out. Questions are kindly provided by Eleven Plus Exams (**www.elevenplusexams.co.uk**)

Sequences

These are presented as multi-choice questions. You will be given a series of diagrams in sequence with one of the diagrams missing. You must select one diagram from a list of possible options that BEST fits the space in the sequence.

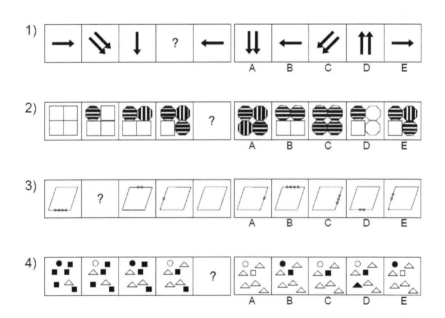

The explanations and answers are opposite.

Sequences Answers

QUESTION 1

The sequence contains two discrete elements:

1. The number of arrows;
2. The position of the arrows.

It is clear that the number of arrows alternates between one arrow then two arrows and so on. The gap in the sequence must be two arrows thus narrowing down the options to A, C or D.

The position of the arrows is all about rotation. Each position is forty-five degrees (one eighth of a turn) clockwise or, if you think about points of a compass, the sequence goes 'East, South-East, South, *unknown*, West' so the gap must be South-West. The only diagram pointing South-West is option C and that also happens to be an option with two arrows. So the answer is C.

QUESTION 2

The sequence contains two discrete elements:

1. The number of white squares versus striped octagons;
2. The position of the stripes in the octagons.

In each position the number of white squares reduces by one so the missing position should contain no white squares at all and instead should be made up entirely of striped octagons.

There are two options – A and C. If you look at the octagons in the sequence you can see that the stripes alternate vertical and horizontal so the answer requires octagons that also have this alternating stripe pattern. Of the two options available only A fits so this is the answer.

Note that as the octagon is a regular polygon we do not know if the octagon itself is rotating or if just the stripes are rotating within the octagon. In this case it does not matter, but in some questions it might be more important.

QUESTION 3

The sequence contains two discrete elements:

1. The number of little circles;
1. The position of the circles on the shape.

The sequence starts with four little circles. The second position in the sequence is the missing element, followed by two circles, one circle and finally no circles. It would seem therefore that the answer needs to be a picture containing three circles, and in this instance there is only one option being answer C.

It is worth checking the logic of this by ensuring that the position of the circles also makes sense in the sequence. Upon inspection it is clear that the position of the circles moves anti-clockwise so the three circles should be on the right side of the shape. In answer C this is the case so it confirms that C is correct.

Note that sometimes a question like this would provide you with two or more answers with three circles in and you would have to check the position to identify the correct option.

QUESTION 4

The sequence contains two discrete elements:

1. Number of shapes – triangles, circles and squares;
2. Shading of the shapes – either black or clear.

This question might at first appear slightly harder although, on close inspection, it is actually relatively simple. You might think you need to be concerned with the position of the shapes, but this is not actually relevant.

Start by counting the number of different types of shapes in each box in the sequence. Note first that the number of white triangles increases each time and the number of black squares correspondingly decreases. There is one circle every time, alternating between black and white. Therefore we need 5 triangles, one square and one circle. Because of the alternating pattern the circle must be shaded black.

That means the answer must be either B or E. However, answer E has a white square and every box within the sequence contains black squares. Answer B does indeed contain a black square so this is the correct answer.

Related Shapes

These are presented as multi-choice questions. You will be given a pair of shapes that are related and one additional shape. You have to understand the nature of the relationship and then choose a shape that BEST relates to the additional shape.

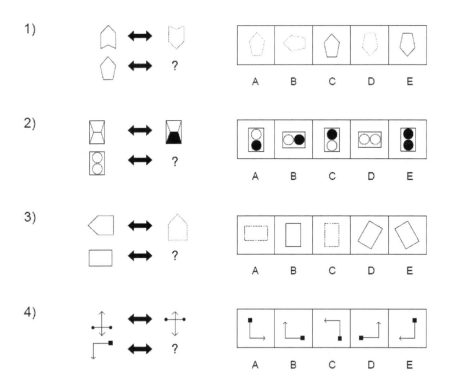

1)

    A   B   C   D   E

2)

    A   B   C   D   E

3)

    A   B   C   D   E

4)

    A   B   C   D   E

The explanations and answers are opposite.

Related Shapes Answers

QUESTION 1

The first arrow (or *primary shape*) in the complete example rotates 180 degrees (or is reflected about a horizontal axis). So the possible answers for the solution to the question must be D or E as they are the primary shape but rotated 180 degrees. The primary shape is made from a solid line but the secondary shape is dotted. Only answer D is dotted so this must be the solution.

QUESTION 2

The answers include two options where the main rectangular shape has been rotated into a *landscape* format. However, the example given does not actually do this so the shape is either kept in the same position or is rotated 180 degrees where symmetry still applies. Therefore at this stage we know the answer has to be A, C or E.

In the example the shape appears to stay exactly the same, but a lower portion is filled in for the secondary shape. The only option where this applies is answer A.

QUESTION 3

In the given example the primary shape is an arrow pointing west. The secondary shape is the same arrow pointing north, i.e. a rotation clockwise of 90 degrees. If the rectangle in the question were to do this then the possible answers are B and C.

As with question 1 above, the primary shape is made from a solid line but the secondary shape is dotted. Answer B is solid and C is dotted so answer C must be the solution.

QUESTION 4

In this question the double-ended arrow crossed by a line with dots on the end has been flipped. Imagine a horizontal line across the middle of it and then spin the pattern over that line. If you apply the same rule to the right angle with an arrow and a square you get answer B.

Shapes & Letters

These are presented as multi-choice questions. You will be given a series of shapes. Each shape is associated with a letter combination that reflects attributes of the shape. The letters act as a form of code. You have to understand what aspects of the shape are represented by the letters and hence choose a letter code that BEST represents the final shape in the series.

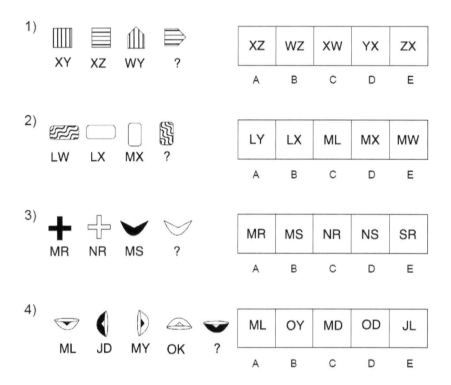

The explanations and answers are opposite.

Shapes & Letters Answers

QUESTION 1

The question shows two shapes, both with stripes running through them, either vertical or horizontal. In the case of the arrow shape, the shape has also changed its orientation, so maybe the square has too, although you cannot be certain. The two squares are identical except for the fact that the stripes change from vertical to horizontal. The code changes from XY to XZ so we can deduce that the second letter is either Y or Z and refers to the orientation of the stripes or shape.

For the second pair of shapes (arrows) the code for the first arrow is also a Y and the stripes are vertical. Both squares start their codes with X so that refers to the shape and hence W must mean 'arrow' so the missing code must be WZ which is option B.

QUESTION 2

The shape is either vertical or horizontal and filled with squiggles or left blank. We can see that the first letter in each code (in this case L or M) refers to the orientation and second letter (W or X) is the fill pattern. By the same logic the missing code must be MW which is answer E.

QUESTION 3

As before, if we apply a logical approach to this, it becomes clear that the first letter (M or N) refers to whether or not the shape has been shaded. The second letter (S or R) therefore corresponds to the shape and hence the correct answer must be NS which is answer D.

QUESTION 4

The letter M appears first for examples 1 and 3, and the only thing the same with them is the combination of white and a small black triangle. Therefore the first letter refers to the shading and hence the solution should start with a letter J as it is also black with a little white triangle. There is only one answer available being answer E. Note that you can reasonably assume that the second letter refers to the position of the shape, but with the answers you have been given it is actually irrelevant.

Blank Squares

These are presented as multi-choice questions. You will be given a grid of squares (either 2 x 2 or 3 x 3) containing simple patterns and shapes. One square in the grid will be blank, and you have to choose which shape from the options provided BEST fits the blank square.

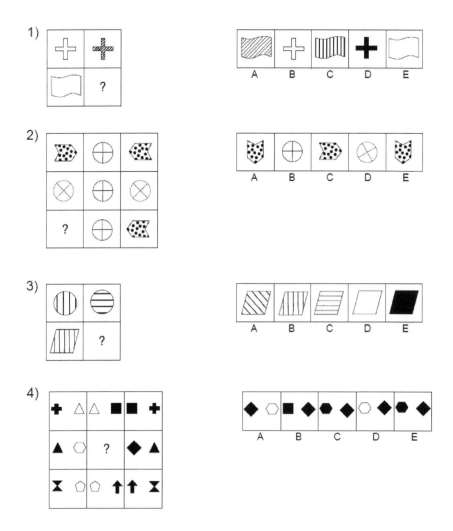

The explanations and answers are opposite.

Blank Squares Answers

QUESTION 1

The 2 x 2 grid contains two crosses, one of which is shaded. Below the unshaded cross is a different shape (a flag), also unshaded. You have to find the shape to go below the shaded cross.

Remember - you have to make a decision based on the information you have been given, and your answer should be the BEST solution. So there could be several possible solutions, but one should be more obvious and appropriate than the others.

For 2 x 2 grids the easiest way to approach them is to consider what changes when you move either across or down and then use these rules to fill in the missing square. If you move right, the shape is shaded. If you move down, the shape changes to a flag. Apply the two rules and you need a shaded flag shape. The answer is therefore A.

QUESTION 2

The 3 x 3 grid contains various derivations of arrows and circles, but it quickly becomes apparent that the pattern of the grid is symmetrical about both horizontal and vertical axes. Hence the correct shape to fill in the blank is answer C.

QUESTION 3

The 2 x 2 grid contains circles and a rhombus, each filled with horizontal or vertical stripes. All available answers are rhombuses. The answer is in the orientation of the stripes. In the top row the stripes move from vertical to horizontal so, applying the same rule, the answer is C.

QUESTION 4

In this 3 x 3 grid the centre square of each row is made up of the elements immediately adjacent, so in the top row for example the centre square contains a white triangle and a black square. Immediately to the left of the white triangle is another white triangle and to the right of the black square is another black square. Apply this logic to the centre missing square and the answer is D.

Similar Shapes

These questions consist of pairs of shapes. You have to choose which shape from the possible answers is most similar to the two shapes given. As with many of the other types of question there could be several possible answers, so always choose the one with the strongest similarity.

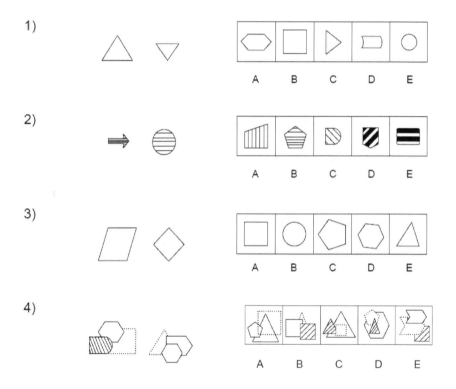

The explanations and answers are opposite.

Similar Shapes Answers

QUESTION 1

This is a very simple question. The two shapes are both triangles and only one answer contains a triangle – Answer C.

Questions like this are sometimes set where two triangles are given as possible answers and perhaps only one is an Isoceles triangle (like these). Another variation would be where there are no triangles given as answers at all and instead most answers contain shapes like options D and E, where some or all of the shape is a curve. There would be only one shape (such as shape A) that, like the triangle, is made entirely of straight lines. Remember, it is always about BEST fit rather than absolute like-for-like copies so make sure you consider lines of symmetry, number of edges, number of fill lines, etc.

QUESTION 2

You might be puzzled by this question as at first glance there appear to be no valid solutions. After all, the shapes shown are an arrow and a circle and neither of those appear in the answer. You will, however, see that the shapes contain horizontal lines. Solutions B and E both contain horizontal elements, but answer E uses thick, black bands quite unlike the arrow and circle's fill patterns. The pentagon is filled in the correct manner so the answer is B.

QUESTION 3

Can you spot the answer straight away? After all, you are given shapes that are at odd angles and are perhaps irregular as well. The common element to both given shapes is the number of sides so the answer is going to be a four-sided shape, i.e. answer A.

QUESTION 4

The two shapes in this instance are actually a combination of shapes but do not let that put you off. They do not each contain exactly the same polygons but they do have one thing in common – that the dotted shape is behind the other two. Apply that rule and the answer is B.

Code Letter Shapes

These questions are similar to the *Shapes & Letters* questions previously, but in a different format. You are given a series of shapes in big squares and each square also contains a two-letter code. You have to understand what aspects of the shape are represented by the letters and hence choose a letter code that BEST represents the uncoded shape.

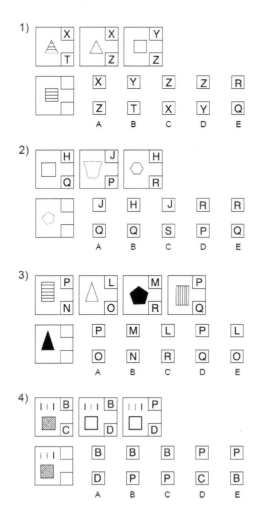

The explanations and answers are opposite.

Code Letter Shapes Answers

QUESTION 1

Hopefully by now you will have started to get the hang of these! X stays the same for the triangles but changes to a Y when the shape is a square. Z means shapes that are unfilled whereas T represents stripes. Therefore a striped square would be Y and T, and hence answer B.

QUESTION 2

This one is much trickier so follow this through with me.

You are only given one useful piece of information and that is the letter H. It is the same in two cases. What is the common element to those? It is the shape outline – solid rather than dotted. Also, the shapes where H is present have both vertical and horizontal lines of symmetry so for now that should be considered as well.

Let us now consider the shape to be coded. It is a dotted shape and, because it is a regular, five-sided shape, it has five lines of symmetry. The way it has been drawn it has no vertical lines of symmetry, but it does have a horizontal line of symmetry. This is clearly different from any rule we can reliably apply to H so therefore, whether it is about symmetry or dots and lines, it is definitely one of the answers with J at the top, i.e. A or C.

Now think about the bottom letter which is different in each case. The only thing that definitely changes from diagram to diagram is the shape. The uncoded solution is a different shape again so the bottom letter should be different to any of the others.

Answer A has a Q at the bottom which is the same as the first example so it may not be right. Answer C has an S at the bottom. This is different again, and even though we don't know what the letter S means (it probably means 'pentagon' but we don't know) we can say that, by a process of elimination, the best fit is definitely answer C.

Note that it is quite common to find questions where you deduce the answer by elimination. Also, don't worry if you cannot be sure of what all the codes mean (like the letter S in this question). This is done deliberately to see if you can follow the logic or if you will be put off by irrelevant information.

QUESTION 3

If your head hurts after that one then don't worry. You'll get used to them, and that's why practice is important.

This one is not quite as nasty, but please note that you are given more information this time – four examples rather than three – so I will walk you through it in detail.

There is only one letter that appears twice so we actually have very little useful information to work with, but don't worry as that's all we actually need! In both cases where P appears the shape is a rectangle – so that must mean that P is a rectangle and hence the top letter represents the shape. At the moment we do not know what the bottom letter means. It probably has something to do with the filling in or shading of the shape but let's see where that leads us.

The unsolved diagram is a triangle, and if the top letter means shape then we need a letter that means 'triangle' and, from the second diagram in the sequence, that would mean top letter has to be an L. That leaves two solutions – C or E – but solution E is the identical lettering to the triangle example, even though the unsolved diagram has changed, and is therefore probably NOT the right answer.

Therefore, again by elimination, it is likely that the correct solution is L and R (answer C) and we can cross check that against our expectations by seeing that in the examples an R on the bottom corresponded to a shaded shape – just the same as our triangle. Hence we can finally say that answer C is definitely correct.

If this is the first time you have tried to do these sorts of problems then you might wonder how you can ever do something like that in 30 seconds (the time you are allowed). Please do not panic. You really can get used to them so you see the logic very quickly, but that is why you need to practise.

QUESTION 4

This one should be OK for you now and you should be able to do it quite quickly. The top letter represents the little black or grey lines, and the bottom letter represents the shading (or not) of the square. Apply that here and the answer is D.

Odd One Out

This category of questions seems, on the surface, quite simple. After all, you just have to spot the odd one out from a series of five simple diagrams or shapes.

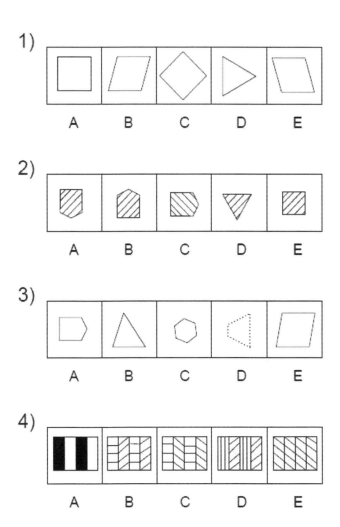

1)

    A   B   C   D   E

2)

    A   B   C   D   E

3)

    A   B   C   D   E

4)

    A   B   C   D   E

The explanations and answers are overleaf.

Odd One Out Answers

QUESTION 1

We have been kind to you with this one. Count the number of sides! All of the shapes are four-sided except the triangle in answer D.

QUESTION 2

Be a little more careful here. The shape is not important. It's the shading we are interested in. And yes they are all filled with diagonal lines so how can there be an odd one out? Well, in one of them the lines slant the opposite way. Answer C is different to the rest.

QUESTION 3

You should see this straight away but I didn't! The first time I did this question I was counting the number of sides then counting the number of lines of symmetry then scratching my head! Then of course I realised it was so simple I had not even spotted it. The odd one out is the one made from a dotted line. It just shows how sometimes you look for the hard or complex answer when actually it might be very basic indeed.

QUESTION 4

Have you just chosen answer A? If so then you have got it wrong! Look again. This question is designed to catch you out if you do it too quickly. Yes you could argue that all the diagrams are made up of columns of little lines and A is the odd one out because it is made from solid black and no lines. But remember the rule about 'best fit'. Every one of the diagrams except one uses an alternating fill pattern across the columns. The one that doesn't is answer E and that is the answer you should give.

Know Your Words

Vocabulary questions can be difficult (even more so for CEM tests), especially if your child is not a big reader. By and large you cannot tell which words will come in tests so, aside from the list we include below, there is not much point in learning huge amounts of vocabulary. Encourage your child to build their own vocabulary list by writing down words that are new to them which they come across at school, in conversation, on the TV or in books, especially if their vocabulary is somewhat limited at the moment.

What your child needs is a broad enough vocabulary so at least they understand the questions. The best way of ensuring this is that they keep reading a lot, at a level that stretches them somewhat. Failing that, there are certain words that do seem to come up regularly in the tests set by the major publishers so on the following page we have listed 132 'tricky' but important words (equates to 12 per day for 11 days or 12 per week for 11 weeks and can be used alongside Anita's tutoring action plan). Some are just difficult, but some are included to see if your child can spot the difference in spelling/sound/meaning. Actually, some questions are set purely to check whether they *can* spell. An example of this style of question is the 'three letters missing' type of question such as (fr[act]ion).

Do not get too frustrated with your child if they do not always know the meaning of words. One school in our area has been known to use the word *grouse* in exam questions. We all know it is a type of bird (although your child may not), but how many people also know it is a verb meaning 'to complain or moan'?

TRICKY LANGUAGE

The question setters like to play tricks with words to further examine the child's ability with vocabulary and meanings. The English language is full of words that mean different things but sound (and sometimes are spelt) the same. Here are a few examples.

In one of the Letts papers there is the word *pail* (an old word for bucket) which is different to the word *pale*, meaning colourless or whitish. For example, when you get sick your mum might say you look pale, whereas if you are at your granny's house she might ask you to fetch the pail from the garden.

Nouns/Verbs sometimes have different meanings. Look at the difference between *a contract* and *to contract*.

- an agreement between two or more parties for the doing or not doing of something specified (noun)
- to draw together, make smaller or shorten: for example: *to contract a muscle (verb)*

In questions where you have to find another word in a group or a similar word it is very important to notice whether it is a noun or a verb. That way you can eliminate many of the other words.

Other common examples of the same word (with the same spelling) being both a noun and a verb include *hamper*, *hound* and *grave*.

There are also words that are spelt the same but have different sounds depending on meaning. How about entrance? This is where context is important. All you can do with Verbal Reasoning is look at the surrounding words.

As a noun it means a way into somewhere. For example your front door is the main entrance into your house. What you may not know is the use of it as a verb when it means 'to put into a trance' so, using it that way, you might read in a fairy story that, 'The mermaid planned to entrance him.'

Then there are words that have the same sound but different spellings and different meanings. *Right, write* and *rite* are all spoken the same way but have completely different meanings.

There is a particularly difficult type of question where you are given two groups of words and you have to find a single word that links both groups.

For example, you might be given the following two groups:

- Interval, wait, duration
- Wand, magic, conjure

The two sets of words have completely different meanings so what is the common link word? *Spell.*

Synonyms and **Antonyms** can be tricky

Enrol and *enlist* are examples of synonyms as they have similar meanings whereas *hamper* and *assist* are examples of antonyms as they have opposite meanings.

Try these. Are these synonyms or antonyms?

- Myth and fable?
- Dense and sparse?
- Frugal and economical?
- Taut and slack?

Try and pair up more of the words on the following page and notice if they are nouns or verbs.

132 'tricky' words to research – (12 per week for 11 weeks)

Adhere	Deviate	Hinder	Priceless
Adjust	Disconnect	Hostile	Prohibit
Allure	Dismal	Hound	Prosperous
Apex	Disperse	Imperative	Pursue
Apparition	Divert	Industry	Reactor
Apprentice	Doe	Initial	Regard
Beret	Drey	Labour	Revere
Bind	Drudge	Latter	Rigid
Bland	Economical	Leveret	Rural
Blistering	Elapse	Magenta	Salute
Bolt	Elevate	Meandered	Saunter
Bonnet	Enlist	Meteorology	Scorn
Brittle	Enrol	Microbe	Scribe
Brook	Entrance	Migrant	Slack
Castanets	Erratic	Millinery	Sonnet
Cease	Escort	Miserly	Sparse
Compact	Fable	Modest	Spectre
Compute	Falter	Moorland	Surge
Conceal	Flee	Myth	Surplus
Confine	Foliage	Nourish	Sustain
Contract	Former	Novice	Synonym
Coppice	Fortify	Orb	Taut
Copse	Fraction	Pact	Tendon
Crater	Frugal	Pail	Tepid
Cultivate	Fulfil	Panorama	Throng
Cygnet	Fungi	Perpendicular	Torrent
Dawn	Girth	Petite	Trade
Debris	Gosling	Pew	Trait
Decipher	Granite	Placid	Traverse
Defer	Gratified	Plumage	Vague
Dense	Grave	Portion	Valour
Detach	Grouse	Possess	Vast
Detain	Hamper	Preserve	Victor

Next Steps

We have now reached the end of this section. You have seen examples of the different types of questions and hopefully have understood the need for practice and guidance. You now need to buy packs of papers and do as many as possible. Eleven Plus Exams kindly supplied the non-verbal reasoning questions you have just tried so log on to their website at **www.elevenplusexams.co.uk**. They have lots of further examples for you to try and can also supply you with practice papers.

The website aims to give you, as a parent, impartial advice on preparation, techniques, 11+ exams in your area and preparation material based on actual experience. The largest forum in 11+ in the UK is moderated by over 20 experts including parents, experienced tutors and authors who collectively give support both before the exams and for those parents who are also unfortunate enough to have to appeal the decisions. The website also serves as a notice board for 11+ mock exams, 11+ intensive courses and 11+ long term courses in the country as well as hosting an extensive 11+ bookshop.

What else you actually do next depends on your situation: time available, requirements of schools you are applying to, ability of your child, etc. We have set it out in more detail in the following section, but as a minimum you need to find out exactly what form of test each school sets, make sure you know when the tests are happening, do whatever is necessary to best understand your child's abilities and limitations so you can make an informed decision about how much additional help to get for them and find out about tutoring options in your area.

If you think you will drive much of the practice and tutoring yourself then familiarise yourself with the tutoring action plans later in this book, order the relevant materials and decide when you are going to start.

They can because they think they can – Euripides

C. Ready, Steady, Go!

You have decided which schools to apply for. You have found out the basics – what they test, when the exams will take place, etc. What do you do next? That is what this section of the book is all about. It provides you with a range of resources that can help you take your child through the whole process.

Recommendations of Papers and Tutoring Action Plan

The first thing that you need to know is where to go for books, practice papers and further information. I (Anita) have already mentioned Eleven Plus Exams, but through their website (**www.elevenplusexams.co.uk**) you can obtain in-depth reading around the 11+ topic, and they also have details about the state grammar schools region by region. They have an online shop and offer downloads of a variety of practice questions.

There are a wide range of published practice papers available to buy here, or if you prefer you can have 'Lessons in the Post' (**www.lessonsinthepost.co.uk**) – essentially a form of distance learning for your child.

The **www.athey-educational.co.uk** website also provides a lot of good information and resources. Their practice papers 'Secondary Selection Portfolio' are also of a good standard. You can also peruse **www.11plusswot.co.uk** and **www.bofa11plus.com**

Most of the time I find that the cheapest place to buy practice papers is Amazon, but if you are going to buy several then ask your retailer if they will do you a bulk buy deal.

There are a number of places on the Internet where you can try free questions or can buy practice questions online. For non-verbal questions and practise for computerised testing try **www.atestingtime.com**; the best scores can be viewed on the website so your child will know they are doing well if their name appears here!

If you have time (11 months or so) you may enjoy working slowly through the four techniques books by Susan Daughtrey (published by Childs World Education), with detailed explanations and GL type practice questions. Her follow-up practice papers show which techniques need further practice as the answers are cross-referenced with earlier books.

Peter Williams (PJW Education) has created some 'Discover' and 'Develop' verbal and non-verbal reasoning books with explanations and exercises with multiple choice answers. These include the most popular type of (GL type) questions.

The Bond Papers are best for learning how to do the questions as they explain the answers in great detail. If you have left the 11+ until the last minute these are a very good idea, especially if mums and dads are struggling to work out the answers!

For some quick explanations, if you have not already done so, look at the verbal and non-verbal reasoning section (the previous chapter) of this book. I have briefly explained all the core verbal techniques together with non-verbal examples from **www.elevenplusexams.co.uk**.

Your final practising should be with the Letts and GL papers (GL has taken over from NFER). These are the ones that, in my experience, are most like the real exam papers. That's probably not surprising as GL set 90% of the school exams!

If your child is going to take a CEM style exam make sure you buy CEM style papers and (in the action plan below) replace the final GL assessment papers with CGP CEM papers.

By now you may have ordered some practice papers. If you have not ordered any papers yet then take a look at the following plans and details of which papers to use. You should also book a place at a local mock exam (see **www.elevenplus.co.uk** for list of local centres). We can help if you are in the London/Surrey area (see our website).

Action Plan – Eleven Plus in Eleven months

Keep it in perspective... 'Today is a gift – that is why it's called the present'.

Great! You have left yourselves enough time so you have a chance to make the learning process enjoyable; dads working out non-verbal questions with their daughters, hot chocolates in a local café with mum playing word games to learn vocabulary, interview 'games' (please see this section later) in restaurants... OK, so not a patch on swimming, bowling and ice-skating, but with careful thought and rewards the experience does not have to be painful.

Even if you are going to attempt all this yourself without a tutor I suggest you follow broadly the same process as I do with my pupils. I start by introducing them to verbal reasoning as initially it feels a bit more normal and less intimidating than non-verbal. After a few weeks of learning hints and tips, with a little homework to practise the more difficult techniques, we work through some practice papers. Then we move on to non-verbal techniques followed by the corresponding practice papers again. The final term is spent doing 'timed papers', gradually working to tighter and more realistic timescales, but by this stage the children should be confident in their techniques, and as a result they generally start to enjoy the challenge.

Action Plan – Eleven Plus in Eleven Weeks

Eleven weeks is a fairly intensive and ambitious timescale if you and your child are new to all this, but if your child is prepared to work and you are prepared to help them (almost) every day then you can still achieve a lot. Note that for the CEM exams this will need to be modified using a variety of Bond and CGP materials, remembering that the CEM exam includes numerical reasoning and comprehensions, etc. Please read the CEM article for more details. The CGP materials are quite tricky so leave them until last in place of the GL papers. Here is what I suggest you do for a GL style approach:

1st week: You should have already ordered some practice papers, but if not then do so immediately. Use the previous chapter of this book to familiarise yourself and your child with each type of verbal question. Practise free online tests. As mentioned previously, find out about mock tests in your area and book a space at one.

2nd week: Go through the non-verbal part of the previous chapter to familiarise yourself with the various techniques. If you have not yet obtained practice papers then make use of online resources to practise any question types that are a particular struggle.

3rd week: Bond pack 1 (verbal and non-verbal = 8 papers). Alternate verbal and non-verbal on a daily basis. I suggest only do six days a week and give yourself and your child one day off. Start with no more than ½ a paper at a time unless your child is coping really well. Mark them carefully, and see if your child can see why they have made mistakes. If necessary, go through any wrong answers with your child, gently explaining the errors and helping them to understand how to do it correctly. You will gradually see a pattern emerging that will show you which types of questions they are struggling with the most.

4th week: Bond papers pack 1 cont. (alternate reasoning types).

5th week: Bond papers - as above.

6th week: Bond papers pack 2. Your child should by now be able to do a whole paper, and you can start to time them (give them too long initially) to put them under some time pressure (4 papers a week plus time for marking and analysis).

7th week: Bond papers pack 2 continued. Practise timed sections such as 20 questions in 10 minutes.

8th week: Letts papers/CGP papers. By now the aim should be to create exam conditions, i.e. the right amount of time. If the papers allow for 30 seconds a question then force them to move on to the next question after 30 seconds. Initially they will hate this, but it really does help build up a sense of urgency as some children simply will not work fast enough otherwise.

9th week: Letts papers continued.

10th week: GL papers (4 packs over 2 weeks).

11th week: GL papers continued.

If you have worked through all the above, gradually ramping up the pressure until your child has spent two weeks working through the GL papers in near-exam conditions, then the chances are you will have a pretty good idea of what they are capable of. If they have done a mock test that will have felt even more like the real thing.

Action Plan – Eleven Plus in Eleven Days

There is no doubt about it - if you are going to try and prepare for an exam in eleven days then you have a very hard and potentially stressful task before you. This only really makes sense if your child is very bright anyway and just needs to familiarise themselves with the question types. They will always do better if they have longer, but if this is all the time you have got then here's what to do (assuming you have bought the relevant papers).

Day 1: Verbal Reasoning examples from this book.

Day 2: Non-verbal reasoning examples from this book.

Day 3: Bond Pack 1 Paper 1 Verbal (1/2 paper at a time)
Work through wrong answers in detail.

Day 4: Bond Paper 1 Non-verbal (1/2 paper at a time)
Work through wrong answers in detail.

Day 5: Bond Paper 2 **timed** Verbal (1/2 paper at a time)
Draw a line under the question you have reached after 25 minutes. Stop at this point. Mark what they have done. Work out the percentage to give you an idea of their current achievement then continue to work to the end of the paper and mark that.

Day 6: Bond Paper 2 **timed** Non-verbal – 10 minutes per section (tell your child when they should be on the next section).
At the end, work through any missing questions and then any wrong answers.

Day 7: Bond Paper 3 verbal - whole paper timed (tell your child what question number they should be on every 10 minutes).
Go through wrong answers in detail.

Day 8:   Bond paper 3 non-verbal - whole paper timed (with your child wearing a watch). Tell them when they are half way through the time.

Any extra days/weekends complete Bond Papers from Pack 1 and Bond pack 2

Day 9:   GL paper 5 – (pack 2) verbal; GL paper 5 - (pack 2) non-verbal, timed. This is at least 2 hrs work.

Day 10:   As above with the next 2 papers.

Day 11:   As above with the next 2 papers.

If you have enough time spread the work out for days 9, 10 and 11 over slightly longer and complete the GL papers. If you have a month, then include the Letts or CGP papers after Day 8 and before the GL papers.

If at all possible aim to fit in at least 25 hours' work in order for this to be most beneficial.

Eleven Plus at the Eleventh Hour

Personally I think that eleven days is as much of an 'eleventh hour' situation as any child can reasonably deal with, but whatever your circumstances and however last minute this is, the most important advice is that the child MUST at least be familiarised with each type of question. There is no spare time in these exams for them to think about what they have to do. The response to each type of question needs to be near instinctive so a little bit of practice of every type of question is better than lots of practice but only some of the question types.

Read through my verbal and non-verbal reasoning examples and practise as many online papers as you can. If you only have time left to work through a few practice papers then buy the GL papers – but most of all... don't panic! Read the later section of this book called 'Missing Piece'. You probably need it more than most!

Exam Day

'You are all winners, each and every one of you.' - Tom Wells

There is no easy way of putting this. The exam day can be a pretty stressful time for parents and children alike. Like it or not, it is probably the culmination of months of planning, work and serious commitment. If you are applying for multiple schools then you are going to face this several times over. Clearly, everyone deals with it differently, and your level of stress will depend in part on your personality, in part on your perception of your child's ability versus everyone else's and in part a reflection of the school situation and the competitiveness in your area.

The most important thing of all is that even if you are feeling almost ill with worry (and I have seen parents who are) you really must not transfer that to your child. It will just make things worse. So my practical tip here is, if you have a choice, make sure the parent who takes the child to the exam is the most laid back and positive of the pair of you. Alternatively, share transport with other parents that you trust.

Our tips for a good day are as follows and are born of experience with our own children and war stories from other parents.

1. Arrive early – there may be 1,000+ cars also looking for a parking space. Why not go really early and have breakfast/lunch first?
2. Make sure your child wears a watch (if digital ensure it is not going to beep every hour) and do not let them take a mobile phone into the room.
3. Go to the toilet before the exam. Your child should go too!
4. Tips for the child:
   a. Work as fast as you can without making silly errors. You should by now have practised enough to have an idea about this.
   b. Use your answer sheet to help you eliminate wrong answers.

c. Do NOT spend too long on any question; 30 seconds for one question should be the maximum. If you find a section difficult go on to the next one.

d. Put a mark in the margin for the ones you leave out so when you look back you can spot them quickly.

e. If you run out of time, fill in anything on the multiple choice paper – you could be right! If there are 5 possible answers then even random guessing means that statistically you will get one question right for every five you guess.

f. If you have time at the end, use it wisely. Go back and check, starting with your most difficult section. Checking means working it out again as if you have not done it before - not having a brief look.

Plan a treat for your child once they have come out of the exam. The chances are they will have worked very hard for at least the last few weeks, and this day is a culmination of all that work. This is a time to reward effort rather than results. Take them out for lunch, go to a movie or buy them a present. If their 'screen' time has been severely limited in recent days and they are desperate to start zapping alien invaders again then buy them a new game – the one they have been going on about for weeks that they say everyone else already has.

The point is simple. Bless them and show them that what matters is that they tried, that you believe in them and that you love them regardless of whatever school they end up in.

Interview Preparation

'The talent of success is nothing more than doing what you can do, well.' - Henry W Longfellow

Not all schools interview everyone that applies. Their rules for this vary considerably, and it is essential that you do not read too much into it if your child is called for interview.

Over the years I have built up a fairly solid understanding of these interviews as I always try and find out from my own pupils what they were asked and what form the interviews take. You will not be surprised when I say that no two schools take quite the same approach, but I can give your child some broad advice.

Know the School

- Visit the school, but don't trust the pupils to give you all the correct answers; a year 7 child may not know about A levels even if he thinks he does!
- Visit the website so you can talk about 'content' rather than 'a nice building'. After a while you won't notice the décor!
- Talk to current pupils. Parents, if you have any concerns you can usually talk to the admissions secretary.

Know Yourself

- Talk about yourself with confidence – achievements, hobbies, interests, pets, recent travel, etc. Is there anything unusual and interesting about you?
- Make sure you have read a good book and watched an interesting film/play/show recently.

Look Your Best

- Make a good first impression – polished shoes and combed hair.
- If you are in mufti look smart but you don't have to be in designer labels!

Keep up-to-date with events

- Record 'Newsround' or any other interesting news programmes and watch them with your parents.
- Discuss current affairs with your parents; know the names of the major royals, the Prime-Minister and any important news article of the month/year.

About You:

- What clubs and activities do you do at school?
- What clubs and activities do you do outside school?
- What awards/exams have you achieved outside school?

Some schools will like a Music or Art portfolio if you are doing a scholarship - see the article about scholarship applications.

Interviewer: **What do you think about animal testing?**

Child: **Animal testing is a terrible idea as they get all nervous and give all the wrong answers.**

Practise talking about yourself in the mirror or to your pets.

Typical Interview questions (from my experience these seem to be widely used):

- Tell me about yourself.
- What makes a successful pupil?
- What motivates you?
- What is your greatest strength?
- What is your greatest weakness?
- If I were to ask one of your teachers to describe you what would they say?
- How has your current school prepared you for this one?
- What do you see yourself doing 15 years from now?
- What has been your greatest achievement so far?
- What book are you reading at the moment, and what do you think of it?
- What film have you seen, and what do you think of it?
- Why have you chosen this school, and what skills will you bring to it?
- What do you do in your spare time?
- What makes a good member of a team?

- What other schools have you applied to? *Tell the truth but make sure you have a good reason to say why you want this one first!*

Fun questions that sometimes get used (discuss during a family meal-time):

- If you were asked to invite a celebrity to your school who would you ask and why?
- What would you do if you won a million pounds?
- Which historical figure would you like to meet?
- What is your favourite period in history?
- What do you think are the three greatest problems facing the world today?
- What has been the most interesting place you have visited so far in your life?
- Which famous people would you invite to dinner and why?
- What one change would you ask the government to introduce into the country and why?
- What do you like best about your mum/dad/sibling?
- What is your happiest memory?
- What do you like/dislike about being a child?
- Tell me about a funny time in your life?
- What's the nicest thing you have ever done for anyone?
- What is the ideal amount for your allowance? How would you spend it?
- What is your favourite thing to do as a family treat?
- What is the funniest thing that has ever happened to you?
- What was your worst moment at school?
- What do you like best about school?
- Is there anything in particular that you remember from a school assembly?
- Do you know why you were given your middle name?
- Does your surname have any special meaning?
- What's your first memory?
- Who is your favourite teacher and why?
- What was the best gift that you remember receiving?
- If you could have 3 wishes what would they be?

- What's the best compliment that you have ever received?
- What do people like about you?
- What is your favourite possession?
- What is your favourite family meal? Do you all eat together? Who cooks?
- What would you like to do when you grow up?
- Where is your favourite country and why?
- What is the most valuable or useful thing that your parents have taught you?

The Interview: *'A laugh is a smile that bursts'* – enjoy your interview then your interviewer will too!

- Practise shaking hands with someone and saying, "Hello, my name is..." Make sure you look at them.
  Ask them if you have a good, confident handshake.
- Speak clearly and tell the truth!
  Do not interrupt, and listen to the questions carefully.
- Think about how you look.
  Try not to slouch or cross your arms over your chest.
  What are your nervous habits? – try not to do them.
- Be enthusiastic and talk confidently.
  Avoid yes/no answers; elaborate on your achievements.

There is clearly a fine line between embellishing the truth and lying! You really do need to ensure your child has a politically correct answer for questions like "Why do you want to come to this school?" as "I don't, but my Mum says we have to apply just in case I don't get into St Jimmy's Elitist Academy for Perfect Children" really is not going to do your child's chances much good. Children at this age are disarmingly honest, and sometimes a little tact is needed.

A TRUE STORY

A boy had a practice interview with his Mum.
She asked, "What are your strengths?"

He replied, "My legs!" and the family fell about laughing (he was good at football so he thought that was a logical answer).

Can you imagine what happened in the real interview when they asked the same question? – The boy started laughing and then had to go on to explain what he had said previously when asked this at home. Luckily the interview panel thought it was funny too. He got a place at the school. How do I know this happened? It was our son!

ARTICLE: School Daze – How to Survive the Application Process
By a 15-year-old girl in Surrey

I know the next couple of traumatic months will unfold slowly and painfully, but I hope I can soothe your inner anxiety... In other words, with my help, you'll survive.

Let's start with open days full of endless classrooms, never ending cloakrooms and the stares of unusually obedient children. The school will appear big and daunting, but it's not nearly as scary as it seems. That is, until the first day of secondary school, where you are completely lost, along with the other ninety-nine year sevens. But don't despair, older students delight in showing you the way, and then using 'lost year sevens' as an excuse for being late for class. Quite frankly, all the schools look the same. Every school has a Maths corridor and an English corridor and a Science block and a... you get the idea. You should focus on what the school specialises in to get the most out of it.

Taster days. Hmmm, if you see a lot of fancy technology, chances are, you'll never see it again. The schools want to impress you because they all want you and, in the case of independent schools, they want your parents' money! Personally, a memory that stands out is a chemistry experiment in which I set fire to my hands. This was not a form of discipline; it genuinely aimed to teach you something about science. I can't remember what the reason was though, so I guess it didn't sink in. On the whole, taster days were a lot of fun, but don't base your entire opinion of that school simply on them. Try to talk to students and teachers to get a more rounded feel for the place.

My mother sent me to a tutor in the months leading up to the exams. She also decided, as well as tutoring, it was necessary to subject me to something so truly horrible that I can barely bring myself to write the next words... past papers! These are the most dreadful things you will ever do, and I had to do five a day, although I did get away with two on Christmas Day. RESULT! I ended up becoming so exhausted throughout the process that there weren't enough hours in the day to fit everything in. My mother, however, happened to become quite good at verbal reasoning while doing my homework. Tutoring is not always necessary, as it is possibly the most infuriating thing you will ever do, but it does definitely help. The tutors know what they are talking about, as they have experience in what is really in the exams.

The actual examinations... fun times. The lead up to the exam is far more scary than the actual event itself, considering you worry not only about the verbal and non-verbal reasoning, but what to wear and even worse, how much make-up to put on! "To mufti or not to mufti?" That is the question. I had a whole shopping trip with the parents to pick something comfortable yet appropriate, posh yet not trying too hard, smart but cool. So basically, we're both never going to be happy with what we get. In the end, a sale at Primark did just fine. The main thing to remember for the exams is that they definitely do not expect you to get 100%, and if you did, you're definite scholarship material. Don't panic if you can't answer all the questions. I know everyone says that, but it's true as the end of the paper especially is made for those annoyingly intelligent robots that seem to know just about everything. CHILL OUT!!

A tip for interviews: Watch Newsround. Everyone does it, and it just about saved my life. Current affairs are a hot topic and, if your school offers interview practice, you can't get enough. Practise with friends, family, over dinner, walking the dog - practice honestly does make perfect. The main thing they are looking for is personality, so BE YOU (unless you are a weird, irritating and generally offensive child... in which case be somebody else!)

The weeks of waiting begin. Your mother becomes an intolerable parrot. "How did you do? What happened? Was it hard? How do you think it went?" This gets old – fast! Every day you run downstairs, sit by the door and stare impatiently out the window for Pat to arrive. One by one, those ominous envelopes drop on to the door mat. Don't be disappointed if you don't have a perfect success rate. It probably means that school just isn't right for you. After each acceptance comes the compulsory ringing the grandparents, cousins, aunties, uncles and, in my case, Great Aunt Agnes. All of this gets even worse when it comes to the time to choose (if you are lucky enough to have more than one offer).

Where do you want to go to school? The private school? You get to set fire to your hands... and stay alive. The state school? You get bigger birthday presents from your parents. The boarding school? INDEPENDENCE! It's just all very confusing.

Ultimately I chose the school that gave out free cookies at the open day ☺

Did you enjoy reading that? I did. I asked a friend of my daughter to write about her experience of the schools' application process, and this article is what she came up with. It's slightly tongue-in-cheek, but I recognise the truth behind the witticisms.

Planner Resources

'Success is the sum of small efforts, repeated day in and day out'.
- Robert Collier

In this section I have created some very simple tables that you and your child can use to track progress.

Individual Pupil Planner

Use a table like this to track your child's progress with practice papers. You should start seeing a gradual increase in scores over time. Don't forget to note down any time restrictions you start to apply as well.

Date	Name and amount of paper *e.g. Bond Pk 1 Paper 1* *NVR 1ˢᵗ Half*	Percentage	Areas of Weakness

Parents' planner

The table on the next page should be used to list school details for open day and application form submissions. It is so easy to miss one of these so write it down, cut this out and stick it up somewhere prominent. Then cross them off as you make the visits or send the forms.

Name of school	Address of school	Phone number	Taster Day date	Open Day date	Date of Application submission	Photo needed (y/n)	Scholarship form sent if applicable*	Bursary form sent if applicable	Entrance exam date	Scholarship test date if applicable

* Additional Requirements – sometimes a portfolio is required for Art or Music scholarships. Normally you do not submit this in advance but instead take it with you to the audition, trial, interview or test.

Do not anticipate trouble or worry about what may never happen. Keep in
the sunlight.
Benjamin Franklin

D. The Missing Piece

The Missing Peace

The missing 'piece' is 'peace'. Many people, pupils and parents alike get worked up about the 11+ process, and it is essential for the mental and emotional wellbeing of you and your child (and the rest of your family) that you keep everything in context and maintain a degree of peace. Your child will pick up any changes in your demeanour very quickly so guard your heart and mind, thus protecting those closest to you as well.

It is important that your child believes in themselves and remains confident even if the evidence (practice test marks) shows otherwise, especially if there are several months until the entrance exams. You also need to trust the school to which you are applying. If they say, "No," then usually that is the right answer. There is no point in your child getting into a school by the skin of their teeth through sheer hard work rather than underlying ability. Once there they will always be struggling to keep up and will therefore be miserable. You need to trust the school to choose your child if they are right for that place.

You can help your child remain confident by encouraging them not to get involved in conversations about schools with their friends.

Tell your child:

- Do not listen to other pupils' opinions about schools.
- Do not listen to other pupils' opinions about 'you'.
- Think about what you *can* do rather than what you *can't* do (positive thinking).
- Relax before bed so your mind isn't buzzing – especially leading up to the exams.

You will find that the 11+ process is an emotional and even 'spiritual' journey, especially if you are a 'faith' family. It is positive for both parent and child to have an ongoing dialogue about their feelings and ideas, and it is healthy to use this time to take stock of your child's abilities and preferences.

At this age children are changing quickly. As well as their obvious physical changes, children develop a lot in their thinking and approach to life, so parents will need to help them deal with difficult decisions and uncertainty of the future. If you are struggling with this as a parent it might be good to chat with another adult rather than put it onto your child. It is certainly an area that I regularly find parents want to talk to me about.

A Time of Transition; a Time of Transformation

The most difficult phase of life is not when no-one understands you; it is when you don't understand yourself.

This is the age when your child is moving into 'middle childhood'. It is a bit like becoming a chrysalis – but unlike a chrysalis the changes are not hidden away, and you have to help your child work through these emotional, physical and intellectual changes in order to help them transform into the beautiful butterfly that you have always hoped that they will become.

Change is hard for some people including children, especially those who have been in a primary school for 7 years. Moving schools may be the first major change that they will have ever faced. They may have never moved school before. They may never have even moved house before. Some children have merely moved from one class to the next with the same group of friends. Do not underestimate the stress that this imminent transition may cause, and because the uncertainty is stressful for parents too it can be challenging to support your child.

At the same time as any tutoring begins in year 5, your child may have to deal with more complex friendships, peer pressure, the beginnings of puberty, more academic challenges at school and increased independence. It is so important to spend time with your child and just talk – but don't forget to do your share of the listening too! If they don't want to talk, there's always the long car journey where they will have to listen to you - even if they don't respond at first. As well as talking about inconsequential things try discussing their physical and emotional changes. Talk about managing homework and social activities. Talk about hopes and dreams. Perhaps most of all talk to them about whether they are happy or unhappy and why. Take an interest in their friends and what is going on in their lives. Enjoy spending time together so that talking is natural.

Boys in particular need their dads at this time. The following extract is from Steve Biddulph's superb book *Raising Boys*, published by Harper Thorsons. He recognises the difference between boys and girls in their learning. School can be challenging for boys who do not want to sit at a desk and learn, and the input from dads doing something other than 'helping with homework' is vital.

> *"From an emotional viewpoint, the father is now more significant. The boy is ready to learn from his Dad, and listens to what he has to say. Often he will take more notice of his father. It's enough to drive his mother wild!*
>
> *This window of time ... is the major opportunity for a father to have an influence on (and build the foundations of masculinity in) his son. Now is the time to 'make time'. Little things count ... working on hobbies or sports together for the enjoyment of doing it ... This is when good memories are laid down that will nourish your son, and you, for decades to come."* [1]

Most children will experience fears and anxieties when thinking about the next stage in their schooling, and you will need to learn how to respond to these. You may start noticing that your child is under pressure if they become more irritable, less tolerant with their friends, attention-seeking, not eating or sleeping so well or complaining of headaches and stomach aches. To children at this age you still have all the answers so make the most of it - encourage them and help them take some responsibility for resolving situations under your close guidance so that in the future they will be able to do it themselves.

---

[1] Reprinted by permission of HarperCollins Publishers Ltd © 2003 Steve Biddulph

Choosing a selective school does add an extra pressure, and for that reason many parents do not choose this route – wanting their children's childhood to be as carefree as possible. Keep a check on yourself or ask family members to help you keep it in perspective if you feel that things are spiralling out of control. It is too much for a child to maintain a couple of years of tutoring, endless papers a week and stressed parents to boot!

However much you may want a particular school, do not turn into the mad mother in John O'Farrell's hilarious and uncomfortably perceptive novel 'May Contain Nuts' (a great read but maybe not while you are going through this process). [2]

> *'While our daughters were having tuition on Saturday mornings, we would meet up like this in my kitchen and debate the major issues of the day. How many secondary schools are you applying to? Is it true that you can only get into Chelsea College if you can speak fluent Latin? We looked at a lovely secondary school in Calais. The only downside is that Bronwyn would have to get up at four thirty every morning to catch the Eurostar'…"*

Alice, being a petite mother, actually ends up taking her daughter's 11+ exam by going in disguise, not believing that her daughter is capable of passing the exam. Don't try this!

Be aware of your child's emotional well-being. Make sure they always have fun things to do besides school work. Plenty of exercise is important as well.

'Happiness is not a destination. It is a method of life.' - Burton Hills

I would like to give you a few thoughts and recommend some more reading if you wish to use this primary-secondary transition time to review family life. You may be halfway through your time of having your child living at home, and it is always good to stop and reflect. Perhaps you are not sure of the right way forward for your child or

---

[2] From 'May Contain Nuts' by John OFarrell, published by Doubleday. Reprinted by permission of the Random House Group Ltd.

your family as a whole. Your family's well-being is of paramount importance for your child's development and sense of security.

What Makes a Happy child? Is my Child Happy?

What makes a happy *person*? Well, I am generally happy on holiday – I am not tired, I eat well, I don't feel over-busy or over-burdened. I can go outside and enjoy the surroundings. I have time to exercise. I spend quality time with my family catching up on conversations and I enjoy making plans for the future. Wouldn't it be great to be on holiday all of the time?!

There are several clues in the above to having a happy child: healthy eating, healthy sleeping and healthy play (with not too many screens!) In addition, good, unrushed communication and interaction within the family all enable a happy family life. Do you have 'time' in life just to 'be' with your family - cooking, bike rides or just 'sofa-time'?

In Sue Palmer's book *Toxic Childhood* (published 2006 by Orion) she deals with many of the above issues. She then also released an essential guide developing her ideas further called *Detoxing Childhood* (Orion, 2007). *Toxic Childhood* contains considerable research and recommends further reading and useful websites for those parents who would like to look into the various topics in more detail. For the ultra-busy parent there is a summary of her ideas at the end of each chapter. *Detoxing Childhood* 'summarizes the evidence and expands the advice' given in the earlier book but is a quicker read. It is a sad fact, however, that the people who most need to read this book are probably too busy or too disinterested to read it.

Sue's book was born out of a recognition that the modern, intense pace of life is damaging children's development. A child's natural learning process requires more time and space than current lifestyles often allow for. Consequently children's common sense and emotional intelligence is behind their parents' at the same age when they were children. There is a significant increase in developmental disorders, in part because in our modern world children's development is being impaired. There is now a substantial body of research that appears to indicate that the symptoms of Attention Deficit Disorder

(ADD), a developmental disorder, are exacerbated by too much screen time and corresponding decreased interaction with real with people.

In our schools we now see more behavioural problems, emotional problems and teenagers with mental health issues, born out of childhood stress. Changes in play and education are just two factors which are affecting children today. Sue talks about how to 'detoxify' childhood to aid our children's development and sense of well-being.

As a teacher for the past twenty years I have noticed how children have become less well-behaved and less respectful of adults. In her first book Sue highlights three areas where she has seen a deterioration in children's behaviour: The first is learning to concentrate, the second is learning self-restraint (not expecting instant gratification) and the third, children recognising other people's needs.

Personally, I love it when children can learn a musical instrument as the results are not instantaneous and it teaches them important skills for life. Regular commitment to fulfil a goal is essential, as is learning to work at something (other than school work) to build skills for rewards in the future. Sadly, I often see children try an activity for just a term and then they move straight on to something else. When assessing whether your child is happy don't be fooled by them into stopping lessons / activities if they complain. They have to learn to persist with something – try a year or two before they give up. I told my daughter that she could give up the piano... when she passed Grade 8! Now she has achieved that and she still loves playing it, but now it's for fun and relaxation. So many parents say to me, 'I wish my mum didn't let me give up!'

In order to pass an exam to a selective secondary school, children do have to exercise concentration, dedication and understand that they will not have instant gratification; it may be one to two years before they see the fruits of their labours. Don't give up tutoring just because they moan a bit from time to time.

Sue, however, warns against making sure your 'tactics are not themselves likely to damage your child's development' through over-tutoring or hot-house environments. We need to keep it in balance. If you are looking at additional verbal, non-verbal, Maths and English tutoring on top of music lessons, gymnastics, Scouts and so on, be careful. You may have to reduce the number of other activities that they do. My personal belief is that children should not have years of English or Maths tutoring for secondary school selection purposes or they won't keep up once they get into the school. Tutoring, however, would be useful if the children need level 6's for their schools (algebra for example is taught at a lower level in year 6 than on most exam papers) or if there is a specific issue to address.

Where parents too can be sucked into this modern competitive lifestyle it is important to continually evaluate our motives as to why we choose a particular school. The right school for your child may not be the one with the best league table positions, the annual rugby tour to South Africa or the choir trip to Vienna. Instead it is the one where your child will be happiest and will thrive (if you haven't already done so, read the article by 'A Parent' about state vs. private in Part A).

We all want a happy child, and as well as trying to get everything in terms of their education right don't forget that the biggest thing that they want is your love and your time.

What if my Child is not Happy?

Most children are relatively 'happy', but if they suddenly become needy, attention-seeking or withdrawn that may be a sign that there is a problem. It is very important that you as a parent can get to the bottom of whatever is bothering them. If there is also a communication breakdown it may be necessary to involve another party. Your child's schools should always be prepared to listen, but teachers are neither counsellors nor doctors (although sometimes as teachers we do have to take on those roles!) It may be that your child will need to be referred for further help, but please be prepared to ask, as some problems can be harder to solve once a child is a teenager.

The tutoring process is not always right for every character. Some children really do not cope with the increased workload (although most of the time they are OK – they just complain to try and get out of it) and some very bright children who always find learning easy are not prepared to learn reasoning as it is so outside their comfort zone. I taught one girl who would only take Maths and English exams for schools as she was completely derailed by trying to do verbal and non-verbal reasoning. For the first time in her life she was faced with an academic discipline that did not immediately come naturally to her. However, it would have been good for her to recognise that you can't necessarily be good at everything.

Naomi Richards is 'The UK's number 1 kid's coach' and has written *The Parent's Toolkit* (published 2012 by Vermilion) which helps parents with their child's issues from confidence and communication through to friendships and schooling. She offers Skype sessions with children to help them with specific problems. You can also receive her daily tips by email. If you are aware that there are issues that need to be resolved, you may find answers in a book such as the ones above, a parenting course, a teacher etc. Your child cannot and will not achieve their best unless they are happy in themselves.

Elevate Eleven's Response to Children's Wellbeing

If you are in the Surrey area, Elevate Eleven runs 'Secondary School Transition' workshops where we look at specific issues related to year 6 pupils and we also run a variety of workshops leading up to exam time to help with motivation and pressure.

Elevate Eleven regards children's well-being as paramount and we can put families in touch with organisations which can give additional support where necessary. As with all of Elevate Eleven's services, details are on the website.

In summary: Listen, keep things in balance, listen again, go out of your way to do positive things with your child and listen some more. Enjoy! Your children will leave home soon enough so make the most of them being around.

Practical Steps

If you are a family who don't normally talk, start with a meal together or a walk. It is much easier when there are fewer distractions and they can't just disappear to tidy their bedroom. Tidy their bedroom? OK, so our daughter is 18 now and she does occasionally sort out her room in between marathon online social networking sessions or Skype conversations with someone she had just spent all day with anyway!

Go through these words and questions together that are aimed at the child.

- How do you feel today? *Give them options like:*

Happy	Random	Peaceful	Nervous	Fed Up
Worried	Scared	Sad	Patient	Cheerful
Brave	Excited	Confused	Confident	Irritable

- What things are worrying you at the moment?
- Are you anxious or excited about moving schools?
- What are your dreams?
- What do you think your mum's/dad's dreams are for you?
- What do you enjoy spending your time doing?
- What makes you happy?
- What do you not like doing?
- What makes you sad?
- Who do you admire and look up to? *Avoid the trivial.*
- How could you be more like this person?
- Who would you not like to be like? *Think about qualities that you do not like!*
- Have you hurt anyone recently? Have you resolved the situation?
- If you could change something about your life what would you change?

Also get them to think about these issues:

- I need to take more responsibility with...
- I need to be more confident with...
- I need to sort out a relationship with...
- I need to make better choices with...

Your Child's Spirituality

Elevate Eleven's ethos is also about elevating the child spiritually and building their self-esteem, and that role is played by the parent, school, church, tutor etc - anyone who can speak faith, love, acceptance, direction and confidence into the child's life.

For faith families a child's spirituality is not an element of their life that should be overlooked at times of transition. Transition is a stage of life when faith can be triggered because it is often a time of intense searching. It can be then that a child can seek comfort and guidance in their faith and the faith example modelled by their families.

I mentioned that for my daughter the school application process was a spiritual journey. She was accepted into her/our first choice school (two days after her friends – what was happening there?) on the same day as her grandmother died. She then proceeded to turn down the scholarship exams that she had been called back for at the other schools being confident that she had found the right school – the one that she had been dreaming and (literally) praying about for the past two years. I am well aware, however, that it is not always that simple.

According to a friend of mine, with a Master's in Theology specialising in children's faith and spirituality, faith needs to be modelled by the parent in order to develop deeper spirituality. "This gives the child the opportunity to develop faith as a result of observation, imitation and being accompanied on their spiritual journey by others whose faith is further developed than their own"

Whatever your understanding of 'spirituality', experience is essential for spiritual growth and the development of emotional maturity. I talked to a year 6 girl recently who has narrowly missed getting into a couple of grammar schools. She needs to be taken on a journey to accept that the wonderful school that did accept her is still a good place for her. She is having to learn the hard truth that the message of 'work hard, then you will get what you want' does not always apply, especially in this day and age when people work hard at university to get a good degree just to find that they are out of work at the end of it. What messages do we give our children to help them to make the best out of life's situations?

A Time to Reflect

Here are some thoughts for you if you're having a tricky moment. Everyone responds to such gems of wisdom differently, and what will be helpful for one may be irrelevant to another. If you have a deep religious faith you are more likely to gain encouragement from, for example, Biblical texts (some included below). You may prefer some of the other quotes I have listed that focus on self-belief or those that emphasise positive thinking. Whatever your preferences, print out quotes and verses that mean something to you and pin them up in obvious places so you keep finding yourself reading them. It's amazing what a bit of positive reinforcement can do for your state of mind.

- *Believe with all your heart that you will do what you were made to do.*
  - Orison Swett Marsden

- *Do not anticipate trouble, or worry about what may never happen, keep in the sunlight.*
  - Benjamin Franklin

- *So be strong and courageous. Do not be afraid and do not panic before them. For the Lord your God will personally go ahead of you. He will neither fail you or abandon you.*
  - Deuteronomy 31:6, New Living Translation

- *Self-trust is the first secret of success.*
  - Ralph Waldo Emerson

- *They can because they think they can.*
  - Euripedes

- *Success is the good fortune that comes from aspiration, desperation, perspiration and inspiration.*
  - Evan Esar

- *Once you replace negative thoughts for positive ones, you'll start having positive results.*
  0- Willie Nelson

- *Summing it all up, friends, I'd say you'll do best by filling your minds and meditating on things true, noble, reputable, authentic, compelling, gracious - the best, not the worst; the beautiful, not the ugly; things to praise, not things to curse.*
  - Philippians 4:8, The Message

- *The pessimist sees difficulty in every difficulty. The optimist sees opportunity in every difficulty.*
  - Winston Churchill

- *First tell yourself what you want to be and then do what you have to do.*
  - Epictetus

- *The road to success is always under construction.*
  - Anonymous

- *To climb steep hills requires a slow pace at first.*
  - William Shakespeare

- *And we know that in all things God works for the good of those who love Him.*
  - Romans 8:28, New International Version

It is worth pointing out here that school success is not a prerequisite to a happy and fulfilled life. Most of you would say that what you want more than anything else for your children is for them to be 'happy'. Whilst a good education can lead to a better job and hence a stronger financial position, this 'worldly' success does not in and of itself equate with a 'happier' life. We have a relative who, despite being bright, did not do well at school because he was totally disinterested. After leaving school he did various bits and pieces but eventually got himself on a London Ambulance service training course. He is now a highly regarded paramedic living in New Zealand. He loves tearing around the roads of rural North Island saving lives, and he and his wife have a phenomenal quality of life over there. They are as 'happy' as anyone we know and are a lesson to anyone about the importance of keeping this schools issue in context.

Having said all that, you are probably reading this book because you want to do all you can to help your child do well at school. After all, success at school does at least open up more options. So, if you find yourself having a bit of a 'wobble' then I advise the following:

1. Remember you are not alone. Many other parents will feel the same as you, even if at the school gate or class coffee morning they appear to be strong and positive. Often it's an act; so don't be too hard on yourself!

2. You need to give yourself brain space by being healthily distracted by other things, so get stuck into hobbies and activities that consume your thinking, at least while you are concentrating on them.

3. Avoid people who talk about school applications incessantly. We got to a point where it seemed to be the only topic of conversation wherever we went and we actually had to ask people if we could please change the subject!

4. Set yourselves rules about when you will and will not discuss it. If you and your partner go out to dinner then agree in advance that you will not speak of anything to do with school choices or, if you need to use the time to discuss one aspect, then agree that you will talk about it first and by the time the main course comes you will not speak further of it that evening. And never, ever discuss it late at night!

5. Do not walk this by yourself. You really don't have to. Speak to someone who has lived through it and therefore understands how you feel, but avoid the pessimists. St Paul had a friend whose original Hebrew name was Joseph but the other apostles called him Barnabas which means 'son of encouragement' (from the Greek *paraklesis* meaning encouragement, comfort, consolation). Do try to talk to people who have a 'Barnabas spirit' because they are the ones who will help you feel better and, more to the point, the opposite type of individual will simply make things feel worse so choose your counsel wisely.

6. Keep your options open. Clearly you need to try to avoid putting all your eggs in one basket as that is going to put huge pressure on you and your child. Apply for a range of schools with differing acceptance criteria so that whatever happens you will probably have at least one good choice offered to you. I find that some parents are frustratingly intransigent about school choices - insisting on one particular school for their child, unwilling to accept the idea that they may not get in there or that other schools could be just as good and hence will not consider other options. I have known children who

have ended up with no school place as a direct result of this attitude. If you are struggling to come to terms with 'who your child actually is' then look up Emily Perl Kingsley's story *Welcome to Holland* (widely quoted on the internet). It was written as a way of Emily explaining what it was like to have a disabled child, but its key point (that Holland is as nice as Italy – just different) can equally well be applied to school choices and accepting your child for who they are.

7. Finally, remember that children are remarkably adaptable and for the most part will quickly settle into a new environment. More often than not, whatever school they end up in, they will soon say they are glad they are there, rather than somewhere else!

A Whole New Perspective

I want to finish this chapter with a superb and thought-provoking article by my good friend Sam Laurie. Sam took a different perspective on this whole subject and dealt with it by going travelling! We will not all do what she and her husband did, but be inspired and dare to think outside the box.

ARTICLE: The World Outside School
By Samantha Laurie. Samantha Laurie writes on parenting and education for The Richmond Magazine and other publications.
She can be contacted at **samlaurie@btconnect.com**

What if this month instead of stockpiling revision guides, stressing over tutors and casting a resentful eye over your remaining holiday entitlement you were making plans to take the kids out of school and travel around the world? You wouldn't be alone. Recession, redundancy, an educational landscape that has come to resemble a sprint hurdle of assessment and cramming has forced many to wonder if a year out of the system seeing the world beyond would be a better *preparation for adulthood than another A*. But can anyone do it? Can children really miss a year of school without adverse consequences?*

Five years ago, we took our three children, then aged 10, 7 and 6 on a four month trip around South America and Australia on a journey that began in the Galapagos Islands and ended in the vast red sand dunes of Western Australia. We'd long talked about it and now we were at the perfect stage - pre-secondary school, post-stroppy toddler. With a son in year 5, playground talk was already charged with secondary schools and tutoring and a yawning awareness that the future would be dictated by school work and exams. With six weeks planning and the blessing of the children's state primary schools which whilst unable to guarantee their places gave us quiet reassurance that all would be well, we gulped back the fear and packed our lives into two trolley bags.

It was the best thing we have ever done. Educationally we set out with the best intentions. Each day the children wrote in their journals, an experience regarded by all three with abject misery. Now these are their most treasured possessions, a family folklore of quirky observations and photos. Three weeks in I dumped the pile of untouched verbal reasoning workbooks in a bin at an Argentinean campsite. It was a significant moment. Now when I look at their journals I wonder why I worried. They learnt all sorts of stuff: they know why kangaroos hop; why there are 13 species of finch but only one species of human on the Galapagos; why human embryos have three kidneys, fur and gills. They learnt how to light a fire, put up a tent, scare off a dingo and order a meal in Spanish.

They also learnt, I hope, that problems can always be sorted. We had our luggage stolen in Chile, but managed to replace things. We nearly lost my daughter on the metro in Santiago when she raced ahead of us onto a departing train, but some alert soul leapt at the 'open' button. When we ran out of petrol 100km from the nearest Argentinean petrol station, we coped with that too. Remarkably, apart from one bout of tonsillitis, none of us fell ill. We even managed to catch 21 flights without losing a single bag.

There were gloomy moments: three weeks of shivering and shooing off bush turkeys in Queensland's worst weather in decades killed off our campervanning appetites for good. Despite the constant attention of two unstressed, unhurried parents, the children rarely ceased bickering: there was always a better seat, biscuit or spade to fight over. But we also debunked the myth that children crave routine. Ours loved the adventure, the change, the unexpectedness and raced into every move with more spirit than we did.

We would do it all again at the drop of a hat. We met people who lived and travelled at the far edge of what seems possible. We saw the most extraordinary sights. Most of all we had this golden opportunity just to be as a family; just us. No school runs, no extra tuition, no commuting, no clubs, no ironing, no urgent emails, no interminable lists of things to do. Nothing except just getting along together. And enjoying the view.

But could we have gone for longer? After four months I was ready for home. Caroline Crier, a French-born voiceover actress and her partner Alan Bayer, a model, had a greater ambition – a year long round-the-world trip with their children aged 12 and 9 on a budget of just £45 a day raked together from a modest home improvement loan and rental on their Surbiton home.

'It was Alan's dream. He wanted to show the children that you don't need lots of money to achieve your dreams; that the world is both vast and small at the same time, reachable. He wanted them to see how children live outside our comfortable existence – that it is not the luxuries in life that make us happy.'

The Bayer-Criers lived frugally. They travelled by local bus and slept in backpacker hostels, tents and cheap cabins. The high points were simple ones, recalls Caroline: lighting a fire to keep warm in an old wooden hut near the Quilotoa crater in the Andes, waking up in New Zealand on sand dunes and skinny dipping in the Atlantic ocean, travelling on the roof of a bus up the Nepalese mountains. The low points – the heat, poverty and harassment of India - nearly drove them home.

They carried books to cover French, English, Science and Maths and agreed that they would find a private tutor on their return if the children had fallen too far behind (they hadn't). In fact, the biggest challenge was not missing schoolwork but discovering that Jules, who'd missed year 8, had lost his school place. 'It was a real test of what we had been trying to teach the children,' says Caroline, 'Trust and be flexible. When things don't work out as you expect, open up to it as a new adventure.'

Teachers and educationalists might be horrified by such a fast and loose approach to education. Stability, continuity and application are the keystones of a good education, we have been taught. Certainly you can't manage a school system if the middle-classes are constantly hopping in and out. But the key objection often cited - that children may never catch up from missed school time - strikes at the very heart of the very unease many parents feel - that education has become a race to accumulate more information, to pass more exams, to display more badges. And that the only place to be educated is in school.

In our case, the children slotted smoothly back into school. My son passed the interview at his selective secondary school by regaling the interviewer with a complex evolutionary tale of cane toad and a snake. All three found that journal writing had improved their literacy. No one it seemed had missed that vital step in long division that I so worried would blight their futures.

The pressure of a school system based on constant examinations and assessments, record numbers of young people without jobs or prospects has left many wondering where those years of application are leading. With university life – once a time-honoured academic space in which to discover how living and studying away from home can alter you – changed irrevocably by debt, the opportunities for assimilating learning have shrunk. Not every family has the flexibility or desire to take their children away for a gap year but everyone deserves the freedom to enjoy the alternative learning and pleasure of a world beyond school.

The talent of success is nothing more than doing what you can do, well.
- Henry H. Longfellow

E. Spoilt For Choice

Navigating Your Regional School Maze

Regional editions of this book give an overview of specific schools in the area to try and help parents understand the options available to them. Although this edition of the book cannot do that, wherever you live there are certain options to look out for and we want to try and help you understand the landscape around you a little better.

The mix of schools available actually varies considerably over the country. For example, where we live in Surrey we have one of the highest concentrations of independent schools in the country. We also have the state grammar system in the east of Surrey, offering academically selective, single sex education to those who can pass the rigorous tests regardless of where you live. In fact, certain state grammar schools near us have become (in)famous for the way in which competitive and ambitious families will move heaven and earth to get their children in. Families can easily afford private education but these schools have such a superb academic reputation that some very wealthy parents choose them and hence spend a lot of time on tutoring and preparation to ensure their child will gain a place.

If you are considering schools that do not operate selection purely on catchment area, the actual distance to the school is only of limited relevance. Our daughter goes to a secondary school sixteen miles away but as it is only a twenty minute train ride and a short walk at either end it does not feel that far away. On the other hand if you are only five miles from a school with no public transport and no ability to take them there every day yourself you may have to discount it entirely (or buy your child a good bike and wet weather gear!)

Even if you are only considering your local comprehensives you may still have a number of choices available. For a start you may have the option of choosing single sex or mixed education. In addition, as an example, if you consider the state comprehensives near us we have those with specialist Performing Arts status, Music status and one which is an 'Enterprise School and 6th form College'. Two schools offer 'out-of-catchment' places to children with demonstrable ability in music, sport, science and technology. There is a girls' school with a specialist technology status and a Roman Catholic school (requires any child to have been baptised as a Catholic) that has Maths and Humanities specialist status.

These specialist statuses do, at least in theory, mean something as they gain additional funding towards certain subjects which is outworked in a variety of ways. For example, one school near us with a specialist music status employs a Brass quintet from the Royal College of Music to teach brass lessons. The school that gets additional funding towards Performing Arts has a full-time Performing Arts co-ordinator whose role is to develop the Arts by involving professionals in running courses and competitions such as the annual Young Performer of the Year competition.

You are probably aware of your local schools but do check out what specialist status they may have and whether they offer places to children with particular ability. If not then remember that even if you were in the catchment area in previous years, unless you live opposite the main gates you have no guarantees about future places as catchment areas change every year. You will also have some idea of the 'reputation' of the schools as voiced by other parents but you cannot, of course, rely on that information. Go to **www.education.gov.uk** and the 'compare schools' link for further information about school choices local to you and then go and visit as many as possible.

When your child is in year 6 you will be sent an 'Information on School Admissions and Transfers' booklet. This contains descriptions of the state schools, school listings and the forms needed to apply for a state school place. **Even if you prefer private education it is very important that you apply for a state school place in case you do not get any of your independent choices.** The form is online so you can keep changing your mind until the closing date.

You *must* look at the school's admissions criteria. There will be a priority for a range of parameters including catchment area, siblings, entrance exams (in some cases), religion or aptitude (special talents).

Information about exam dates for state schools that set entrance exams can be found on the schools' own websites or at **www.elevenplusexams.co.uk**. This website will also explain more about **Admissions Criteria, Standardised Scores** and also **School Appeals** if you do not get into the school of your choice. Please refer to this if you require a greater depth of information than provided here. Your current primary school should give you support if you find yourself needing to appeal.

There are different types of state secondary schools according to how they are funded, but does this actually make any difference to the day-to-day running of the school? This should be something you investigate through school visits, open days and meetings with staff.

Parents sometimes choose 'faith' schools even if they do not attend a church, mosque, synagogue, etc. as the results are often better. When a school focuses on values this can also positively impact the working environment and thus the children achieve more. Parents may also increase attendance at the associated place of worship (even if they already go to another one!) to try and meet the admissions requirements and maximise the chances of being offered a place in a school they perceive to be good.

Academic Focus

If you know that your child is working at a high level in school and is in the top groups then you should consider those schools (whether state or private) that have excellent academic reputations and that set rigorous entrance exams. Do NOT just rely on what the schools themselves say to judge how academically demanding they are. They all want to come across as academically excellent but some will take a wide range of abilities and make the best of what they have and others will only accept very bright children and, frankly, will expect most of them to get straight 'A*' and A's' at GCSE. Those that are most academically demanding generally reflect that in their entry requirements. Many of the independent schools interview children as well. This can be very important and we know of children who did well in academic exams (they passed and were shortlisted) but unfortunately did not interview well and as a result were not offered a place.

Some schools pride themselves on being able to help the very able excel yet are nurturing in a way that enables the less academic child to achieve as well. These schools all, to a greater or lesser extent, make a point of offering places to a broader range of abilities, and hence judging them by league table results is particularly misleading. Value Added would be a more appropriate measure in some instances.

Some schools have sixth forms so it is worth thinking about whether or not you want your child to stay in the same school for sixth form. Near us we also have a state sixth form college that offers a more grown-up experience as a bridge between school and university. Some of the independent schools may be single sex but have a mixed sixth form. When making a comparison do not forget to take a close look at course content and availability. Our daughter, who wants to do Music 'A' level, cannot be in an orchestra at the sixth form college and one of her other preferred subjects is not available there. One school near us offers the option of the International Baccalaureate in place of 'A' levels.

All independent schools near us do set entrance exams. Whilst they will of course use these where relevant to select on the basis of academic ability, some of the mixed ability schools analyse the results in a rather different manner, using the exams to help identify special needs, issues or areas of particular strength and weakness. They use this information to decide whether or not they have appropriate resources to support the child adequately.

What is remarkable is that all of the schools we have visited over the years have a completely different feel about them. We would therefore strongly recommend that once you have narrowed it down to a manageable handful of options you really need to visit schools (see our earlier information on this) yourself. Note that their fees and facilities (not necessarily a close correlation) also vary considerably.

Special Needs

If you are concerned that your child is currently underachieving there may be a developmental reason for this. Dyslexic children learn in a different way so if it is relatively mild and undiagnosed then their needs will not be catered for. This is where you need an Educational Psychologist's report. Please go to **www.dyslexiaaction.org.uk** for more information.

I discovered that our son was dyslexic in year 4. He then received two years of support and was given 25% extra time in secondary entrance exams. As a result of all this he won a place at an academically selective school. For more information on dyslexic schools go to **www.dyslexicschools.co.uk**. 'Crested' is a register of schools known for helping children with dyslexia. See **www.crested.org.uk**.

The Preparatory System and Specialist Schools

Some children probably benefit from staying within the prep school route and then transferring at age 13. Maybe, if you can afford it, your child would benefit from being at the top end of a prep school. This can be particularly the case for boys who generally develop later than girls.

Prep schools are so named because they 'prepare' children for entry to the more traditional 'Public schools'. Nowadays the term 'independent senior school' is more widely used. Prep schools tend to cover the junior age up to 11 or junior/middle school age up to 13. Pre-prep is the 'infant age' where the children are taught by the class teacher. In the prep system children have 'subject lessons' from an earlier age so prep school children tend to have quite in-depth knowledge about things like mountains/rivers, the Battle of Hastings or French verbs and so on all by the time they are 9.

Some private schools only start at 13 years old as they entirely rely on the feed from prep schools. However, many other schools who start children at age 11 will also offer some places to children coming at age 13. Typically in such instances children will have to sit an entrance exam in the autumn term of year 8 which will include Maths, English, a Modern Language and Science.

You may also have highly specialised schools near you and perhaps your child has the sort of abilities that would make them candidates. For example, near us we have the Royal Ballet School, the Yehudi Menuhin School and the BRIT School.

The best place to look for up-to-date, reliable schools' information for state schools is **www.education.gov.uk**. The website **www.Best-schools.co.uk** is also worth a browse. The league tables can be found here as well.

The Independent Schools Council or ISC is very helpful. It represents 1280 independent schools and offers advice on its website **www.isc.co.uk**. Finally, I would encourage you to visit the Good Schools Guide at **www.goodschoolsguide.co.uk**.

Summary

We have tried to give the reader a quick walk-through of the sorts of school options that may be available to you, wherever you live. In some areas there is a considerable choice, and people do have differing opinions about schools' relative academic, nurturing, value-added, sporting or creative capability. Any opinion we offer in this publication is therefore intended purely as a way of assisting you in working through the options and is a reflection of our own experience over the years.

Ultimately you will make your own choices, and you may end up disagreeing with us – so feel free to get in touch via our website… and we trust that you, as parents, will enjoy the adventure of finding your child's niche in secondary education. When you find the right school it will be such a blessing.

We wish you well and we hope that we will have helped to reduce some of the headaches and stress along the way.

Anita and Tim Hill
Claygate, Surrey
January 2015

Contact us at **www.elevateeleven.com**

Bibliography

Biddulph, S (2010). **Raising Boys**. *Why Boys are Different – and How to Help Them Become Well-Balanced Men*. London: HarperCollins

O'Farrell, J (2005). **May Contain Nuts**. London: Doubleday

Palmer, S (2006). **Toxic Childhood**. *How the Modern World Is Damaging Our Children and What We Can Do About It*. London: Orion

Palmer, S (2007). **Detoxing Childhood**. *What Parents Need to Know to Raise Bright, Balanced Children*. London: Orion

Plumbley, N (2008). **Compare and contrast the faith development theories of Westerhoff and Fowler in relation to children**. Essay, The Child and the Church Module, Children's Evangelism and Nurture Dip HE. Cliff College: Manchester University, p3

Richards, N (2012). **The Parent's Toolkit**. *Simple and Effective Ways to Help Your Child Be Their Best*. London: Vermilion

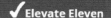**Elevate Eleven**

✓ **Tutoring in N.E. Surrey** – small group verbal and non-verbal, Maths and English lessons with a personalised approach. High success rate without the stress

✓ **Find-A-School Consultancy for the Esher area** – helping you find the 'right' school for your child. Includes a detailed, structured interview with the parents followed by a written report and follow-up conversation

✓ **11+ Mock Tests** – representative tests under exam conditions with individual email feedback based on a comprehensive analysis of the marks

✓ **Workshops & Revision Camps** – interactive and exciting holiday clubs and revision sessions with an emphasis on structured learning to reinforce skills;

✓ **Talk To A Tutor** – free parent talks where the tutors explain the school situation in the local area, present alternative preparation options and discuss individual needs.

 Please see www.ElevateEleven.com or call Anita on 07730 955 699

Anita and Tim can be contacted via the
Elevate Eleven website at:

www.elevateeleven.com

or by email:

info@elevateeleven.com

Elevate Eleven
2 Rosehill
Esher
Surrey
KT10 0HL

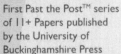